Peace, Love and Jesus:

Greco-Buddhism Antidote for Messianic Judaism

By Thomas Ragland (Gnostic Tom):

2003   The Noble Eightfold Path of Christ: Jesus Teaches the Dharma of Buddhism (1412000130)

2005   Buddha Turns the Kabbalah Wheel: Jewish Buddhist Resonance from a Christian Gnostic Perspective (1412064619)

2009   Jesus Gnosis Story of Simon by Philip (1426913655)

2013   Sermon on the Mount by Jesus (0989251105)

2015   Jesus Gnosis: Ulysses, Dionysus, Baal, and Lucifer (0989251112)

2017   Peace, Love and Jesus (0989251129)

Peace, Love and Jesus

Greco-Buddhism Antidote for Messianic Judaism

A fluffy bunny book by Gnostic Tom (Thomas Ragland)

Thomas Ragland
2017

First Printing: 2017

ISBN-13: 978-0-9892511-2-9

ISBN-10: 0989251129

Thomas Ragland
Nashville, Tennessee

About this Book

You have to be a bit intellectual to even bother to read this. You have to have a history of Fundamentalist faith to really need this. If you went to private school and were told what to think and how to react, this is a gift to you. If you paid for this, send me your receipt and I will pay you back. And tell all your friends.

About Gnostic Tom

Gnostic is a word like erudition, it implies well considered conclusions derived at from personal experience, scholarship in a holistic fashion, the search for patterns and meaning, paradigm shifts triggered from both learning and unlearning. It is my pet word. It is subjective to me and belongs to me and it is a constant in my mind that cannot be altered because other people define the word differently for themselves. A Buddhist word like this, another favorite of mine, is **Dharma***, that collection of truths and concepts that I have found useful for crossing over the various streams of life. If words could label a person, my name is* **Dharma Gnosis***.*

I grew up during the Vietnam War. There were protests of people who opposed war and wanted to **give peace a chance***. These protests were not supported by the church people I encountered. We had to fight the* **godless commies***. It was important for soldiers to be sent for such a noble cause. The people shouting about peace were not Christians. They were flower power drug addict hippies, beatnik Western Buddhists, the alternative counter-culture of lost souls. The churches would hold bonfires where you brought your Satanic music albums to be burned. I kid you not. I was actually invited to one. But it was the voices of popular music and pop culture philosophers that echoed across the minds of those who could see the insanity in the war machine. When I read the words of Jesus in the gospels, I wondered why it wasn't the churches who were on the front line of the peace movement. Peace, Love and Beatles. Peace, Love and Flower Power. Why not Peace, Love and Jesus? Was that not how it all began so many centuries of time ago?*

Questions of why Christianity started out so very extremely anti-Semitic while carrying around Jewish scriptures as being sacred, why Jesus sounds more like Buddha than Moses, and why all of his advice and insight seems to oppose the very concept of the Jewish Messiah, come to haunt the young boy trying to fit in with the Sunday School lessons in a small town Southern Baptist Church.

Reading a lot and writing down thoughts may seem like such a distraction from interacting with the real world out there. Perhaps the pen will prove to be truly mightier than the sword. To collect enough aha moments and paradigm shifts, enough learning and unlearning, follow enough threads through cultures and ages, until with one click of the mouse a published idea will reshape the world. This book is only a seed and it takes an open mind to contemplate, an open heart to embrace, and an open door to then share.

Before Word

We live in such a glorious age of instant information retrieval. You are probably reading this as an e-book instead of as a paperback. Either way, remember you can internet search for any word, any concept, for definition and for further research.

This is a psychological book thinly disguised as a religious or historical study. It is as much about here and now as back then and so far away. If any spiritual text is not about practical insights for making life better, then what use is it? There are too many other things to occupy our time with in the modern world.

I think there are two paths for people who are curious and want to understand how it all fits together, what it all means. These are just for the curious, for most people don't really give religion much of a second thought, even the ones who attend church every Sunday. The first path is Fundamentalism, like the Southern Baptists I grew up around. They like things agreed upon, carved in stone, dates and events and word meanings and a defined and memorized theology. Jesus died in Jerusalem in the year 30 and physically came back to life and physically ascended into the sky. Got to link that back to the Original Sin event of 4004 BC in the Garden of Eden and the theology of blood atonement combined with the misunderstood appropriation of Mystery School mythology, and they can sing songs about the blood of Jesus saving them. The second path is Holistic. It doesn't have one particular label, but is instead a mindset that sees resonances of ideas across cultures and ages, archetypical universal concepts played out in stories and collections of thoughts. For the Holistic, nothing is carved in stone, everything is fluid and its meanings and textures change in the light of considering other ideas. Fundamentalists offer creeds and demand faith. Holistic Minded Seekers offer ideas and suggest pondering them. It goes back centuries, this dance between the two different views. On the one hand, there is the Fundamentalist, being the origins of what became Christianity, the orthodox (only this is right) and catholic (everyone should think this way) apostolic (because it is historical and traditional) Church. On the other hand, there is the Holistic, being *the origins of what was Gnosticism, the fluid creative **mind play** of spiritual ideas including that of Jesus. It is from the Holistic Gnostic side of things that this book is presented.*

The first jhana with applied and sustained thought. The first alternative way of thinking that once you grasp it will stick with you and transform you. A vehicle for escaping their mind trap and rediscovering your path.

This is not a religious book. It is more of an antidote for religious thinking. It is that thread of rebellion that runs through Siddhartha the Buddha not supporting the Hindu priesthood and Jesus not supporting the Jewish priesthood.

While this book can be read for the collection of useful ideas that resonate between Siddhartha and Jesus, between 2500 years ago and 1900 years ago, it may also serve scholars to contemplate the Buddhist influences on the formation of the Gospel story. What does it mean to view Jesus as the Buddha for the Roman world? Stories were created about the supposed travels of an historical Jesus in India before he began to teach. The explanation of this book is much simpler and more believable than any fabricated journeys of Jesus as a child.

Peace, Love

Original Prodigal Son Story

Lotus Sutra 04 - - - - - - - - A young man ran away from his father and lived for a long time in a far away land. Fifty years went by. The older he got, the poorer he became. He tried every direction, begging for food and warm clothing, wandering further and further from home. One day by chance he was journeying close to home. His father had searched for him for years. He was very wealthy. At last the son came to the town where his father lived. The father thought with regret and hope, since he was becoming old and weak, that there would be no one to inherit all of his wealth. He thought, if only he could find his lost son. The son came to his father's gate, but seeing the wealth and power of his father he departed. He went to a poor village to work. The father sent a servant to bring back his son. The son was afraid that he was being arrested. The father seeing his fear ordered that he be let go. He then sent his servants to offer the son a job that paid twice as much as he could make. He then visited his son in disguise, advising him to not be lazy in his work. Later he visited him and told him that he would provide him with everything he needed, adopting him as his very son. For twenty years the son thought of himself as an employed worker. When the father became ill and knew he was about to die, he told his son to take control of his wealth. The poor son managed the wealth, but didn't take any of it, not even the cost of a single meal. Near death, the father arranged a meeting with his relatives and told the story of the son who left home at a young age and came back as his servant. The son was overjoyed at having gained riches beyond anything he could have hoped for.

Luke 15:11-24 And he said, A certain man had two sons: And the younger of them said to his father, Father, give me the portion of goods that falleth to me. And he divided unto them his living. And not many days after the younger son gathered all together, and took his journey into a far country, and there wasted his substance with riotous living. And when he had spent all, there arose a mighty famine in that land; and he began to be in want. And he went and joined himself to a citizen of that country; and he sent him into his fields to feed swine. And he would fain have filled his belly with the husks that the swine did eat: and no man gave unto him. And when he came to himself, he said, How many hired servants of my father's have bread enough and to spare, and I perish with hunger! I will arise and go to my father, and will say unto him, Father, I have sinned against heaven, and before thee, And am no more worthy to be called thy son: make me as one of thy hired servants. And he arose, and came to his father. But when he was yet a great way off, his father saw him, and had compassion, and ran, and fell on his neck, and kissed him. And the son said unto him, Father, I have sinned against heaven, and in thy sight, and am no more worthy to be called thy son. But the father said to his servants, Bring forth the best robe, and put it on him; and put a ring on his hand, and shoes on his feet: And bring hither the fatted calf, and kill it; and let us eat, and be merry: For this my son was dead, and is alive again; he was lost, and is found. And they began to be merry.

Coming home. There is a story in the Acts of Thomas about a prince who went to Egypt on a quest to find a pearl and there forgot he was a prince. He had gotten distracted and trapped in his ignorance. It is the Gnostic myth that we are all from a different realm, a higher place, and we have forgotten. If there is anything we need saved from, it is ignorance. Remembering *(**Gnosis**)* is key. Not faith. Not ideas. Not conformity. Waking up and remembering is the only way. We are each the Prodigal Son who just needs to remember our place and come back home.

Hadrian

Lotus Sutra 14 - - - - - - - - In explaining this sutra, take no delight in speaking of the limitations of any people with their scriptures. Display no contempt for the many ways that the **Dharma** *is taught.*

When you can create stone, pour concrete, you can build roads and bridges and aqueducts and walls with the hard and heavy arches and columns from the imagination of your brightest minds and the brute strength of legions of the world's finest soldiers. All roads lead to Rome, the city of Romance, the heart of the Empire that stretches from Britain to Egypt. There are a few golden moments in human history where it all came together before it all fell to pieces once again. One world under Caesar, united in relative peace and prosperity, progress and a cosmopolitan sense of sharing knowledge across languages and cultures.

When you are a scholar, you hope there are lots of notes about the subject you are exploring. Most of Hadrian's life and adventures are in the dark. Some places and events are only found in memoirs, and what survives future redactors of a history written by Cassius Dio Cocceianus in 222 is sketchy and brief. A few concepts jump out that are worth noting. When he was at home, he was solitary, would read and write. When he was in a group eating, he surrounded himself with intellectual discussions. When traveling, he would attend the festivals and experience the local customs by sleeping in the houses where the common folk lived. When he was with his legions, he would sleep with the soldiers in their quarters. He was directly engaged with exploring life with a curiosity of investigating and inspecting the way people lived, their surroundings, their habits. He did not ride a chariot up above the people. He either walked or road on one of his beloved horses. He was looking for ideas on how to better the lives of the people in the various regions he explored.

Once the war with the Jews had ended, he didn't want to leave Jerusalem in such a state. He banned Jews from coming within viewing distance, renamed the city Aelia Capitolina, erected a new temple for Jupiter, and transformed it into a safe cosmopolitan city, protected under Rome and inspired under Hellenism. The entire region around Aelia Capitolina was renamed Syria Palaestina, in memory of the ancient Philistines who lived in the area before the Jews had defeated them to make it their Promised Land. It was the ultimate "edit undo" button presses. How do you achieve peace for all? You have to repress those who demand peace for only their one little group at the expense of everyone else. In a way you could say that Hadrian was the Prince of Peace who saw to it that Jerusalem at long last saw the end of the violent resistance of Christ-ian (Messianic) Jews.

A lot of Caesars that had come before and would come afterwards were born into the role, related to the previous Caesar, royalty, special. Hadrian was adopted into the role and his successor was adopted into the role, children of humanity. Niccolo Machiavelli in 1503 pointed out in his studies of Roman history that there were "Five Good Emperors": Nerva, Trajan, Hadrian, Antonius Pius, and Marcus Aurelius. Within this subset, Hadrian stands out as remarkable. The expansion conquests of Emperor Trajan in Mesopotamia and Armenia were abandoned, the legions withdrawn. He negotiated peace with Parthia in 121 and suppressed an invasion of the Alani in 135. In Britain where the Roman occupation there was being guarded against attacks, he had a wall constructed in 132 to provide for peace. He was a Caesar who traveled to explore the world, not to engage in battles. He never started a war. He never invaded anywhere. When he traveled to the places where the Romans had expanded, he assisted them with having his legions of soldiers help with construction work, leaving them with smooth roads and running water and relative peace and prosperity. He led out of admiration instead of fear, by example instead of demand, by values instead of mindless rules. While other emperors kept themselves surrounded by guards to protect their lives, Hadrian was beloved by the peoples and the Senate and had no fear of assassination.

He was drawn to Greece, to study with the Stoic philosophers, to attend the Theatre of Dionysus, to explore the concept of establishing a provincial parliament form of government, to complete the construction of the Temple of the Olympian Zeus (the Greek face of his Roman god Jupiter), to complete the Olympieum, and to become admitted to the highest grade of the Mysteries. He was also drawn to Alexandria, that cultural and intellectual hub city of Hellenism linked to the Far East.

*Truce is in effect, all is quiet on the front, we at leisure live in tranquility.   Hadrian was a poet who read and wrote in Latin and Greek.   He had at his command the finest trained soldiers grouped into organized legions, but he negotiated peace when possible.   He had an empire composed of various cultures of people, and he balanced the unity of connectivity with Rome with a celebration of their diversities.   Annuit coeptis, prosperous beginnings, novus ordo seclorum, of a new ordered age, e pluribus unum, the diversity united. Shared prosperity and order, physical design structure, intellectual achievements.   Admiration, charity, the sharing of simple pleasures and   modern   conveniences,   connection,   empowering,   inflaming, Hadrian travelled and ordered the building of libraries, of theatres, of aqueducts and bath houses, temples and monuments.   To bring his world into being a network of civilized peoples with a cosmopolitan connection.   United in the commonwealth of Rome and the intellectual capacity of Hellenism, a **one world culture** of a diversity of peoples living in peace and cooperation, Hadrian's humanist vision for his Empire, along with his love for peace and charity, makes him one of the good Emperors.   If you move the timeline very much backwards or forwards from the time of Hadrian, you see just how tiny was this Camelot window opening.*

*In Star Trek, the Borg would assimilate different species, the collective benefiting from the best qualities of each.   It was this openness to the possibility of encountering something completely foreign that had something to teach, something to offer, some **Gnosis** of experiences unimagined.   Hadrian's big world was one of exploration and assimilation, words in Latin, words in Greek, innovations in construction and engineering, new ideas like public education and democracy, linking the myriad of divine pantheons into one cosmopolitan spirituality, the physical challenges of the Olympic games, the mental challenges of the Mysteries, and the paradigm shifting questions and conclusions of the philosophers.*

Greco-Buddhism

Hanukkah is the December festival of lights Jewish holiday celebration of the Maccabees successfully fighting against the foreign rule of the Greeks. Pure again at last with all these foreign Hellenistic ideas checked. Xenophobia is another word for cultural purity, fear of everything different, everything that would make you question your tradition, your faith, your values, your sense of sacred. Different is profane. Different is Satanic. The lights shine in the darkest days of the year to remind the faithful chosen that the darkness of the pagan world cannot reach their pure hearts.

The Greeks assigned faces (deities) to the passions and forces that drive each of us. These same concepts were to be held by the Romans, just with different names. At the top of the chart was Father Zeus, Jupiter in Rome, the wise organizational ruling force effort. Aphrodite, the goddess of Love, Venus in Rome, was elevated to an importance beside that of Zeus. For what is all of the structure and power without compassion and sharing it with someone you love? Hermes, the god of words, Mercury in Rome, the speed of thought, the magic to convey ideas, to heal, to direct. Ares, the god of violence, Mars in Rome, the power of physical persuasion, of conquering and conquest. We are all composed of pockets of competing practiced effort, the interactions of compassion, speech, and standing up for our personal intent in a conflicting world. We are each a cosmos in which the gods live and act, Jupiter, Venus, Mercury, Mars, revolving around us, each of us being a sun, each a source of light and energy. The ancient Greeks saw people as being related to the cosmos and that by knowing ourselves we could know everything, and by learning about what's out there we can know more about ourselves. This applied to mathematical relationships, to music, to art and architecture, and to the various schools of philosophy. As above, so below.

Greco-Buddhism is this fascinating chemical reaction between West and East, between philosophers and transcendental monks, reason and heart, made possible through the expansion of the Empire of Alexander the Great in 334 BC. The world was opened to trade and cultural exchanges, religious tolerance and syncretism in a living and fluid Hellenism that propelled the Greek speaking world into a *collective of sharing and adapting ideas and spiritual building blocks into new frameworks for thought, new deities, new philosophical schools. From Egypt to India, the Greeks collected and arranged ideas, revolving around the hub of Alexandria, Egypt, the cultural and intellectual center of the world named after Alexander the Great. A fantastic library was collected, hosting the secrets of the known world. The Hebrew scriptures were translated into Greek and many could only read the Greek versions. The Buddhist sutras were translated into Greek, as many Greek colonies were established by the Greco-Bactrians in Northern India. Buddhists were living in Alexandria before the city became the birthplace of Gnostic Christianity.*

*Before the Greeks encountered the Buddha, the Buddha had no face. The Greeks sought out form and context and "the big picture" of how it all fits and works together. What does it all mean? As the gods were given anthropomorphic representations, so the Buddha was given a face. The vague Eastern symbols of wheels and trees and flags and seats and footprints were not enough for the Greeks. The very concept of "large vehicle", of Mahayana, of Buddha being for the world and not just for the few, arose only after the Greek influence began to evolve Buddhism. Milinda Panha is an ancient Buddhist sutra written in platonic style. The Greeks had to see something natural, identifiable, in anything spiritual, for humanity is part of a larger whole, and to know ourselves or to know the whole should result in the same ultimate **Gnosis** (direct understanding) of how it all fits. The sermons repeated must be practical, the ideas relatable in real life. The settings must be believable, real seekers coming to real places to meet a real Buddha, live and in person. Greco-Buddhism propelled the artistic and conceptual development of what was to evolve into Mahayana Buddhism, expanded through Buddhist emissaries that lived and shared the **Dharma** in Greek in Alexandria. While Buddhism had ventured Westward as described in the Rock Edicts of Ashoka, influenced the Skeptics (Pyrrho) and Cynics (Onesicritus), it was precisely in the second century at just about the time we are dealing with in this book that Mahayana Buddhism began to blossom. What the world needs now is peace and love. It wouldn't have been a hard sell in Alexandria in 132. The Christ (Messiah) driven Jews had caused riots since the Kitos War,* *and now the new Messianic pretender, Simon bar Kokhba, was beginning a whole new round in Jerusalem.*

Religious tolerance and syncretism meet Fundamentalist xenophobic exclusivism. The mind expanding cosmopolitan quest for ideas meets the division of the world into us and them, saved and damned, friend and enemy.

Tathagatagarbha

When you first read a foreign word, it is a bit off putting, but after a few of them you discover that people are mostly the same across cultures and languages and ages, from primitives to technologically advanced, from poor to rich. Different experiences and situations, but we all are the same types of minds experiencing the same living bodies with the same basic human traits and experiences and desires and potentials.

Once you can put yourself in the position of the preserved words that attempt to capture a mindset of a person who lived centuries ago in a land far away, who thought in a different language, identified with a different religion, you can bring their thoughts home to your own life and your own modern times.

Read the following as they are, looking up the words on the internet if you like, then read these parables again with the familiar Christian substitutions. For **Dharma**, read kingdom. For Tathagatagarbha, read holy spirit. For klesas, read sins. For buddhagarbha, read angel. For Buddha nature, read Jesus nature. Put it together and it could be an early Christian sermon instead of a Buddhist thread (sutra). Combine enough threads from various Buddhist (Theravada and Mahayana traditions) and Taoist sources, and it could be the original framework for the Gospel story.

Tathagatagarbha Sutra - - - - - - - - It is just like what happens when the honey in a cave or tree, though surrounded by countless bees, is taken by someone who knows a clever technique to first get rid of the swarm. The Tathagatagarbha of sentient beings is like the honey in a cave or tree. The entanglement of ignorance and tribulation is like the swarm of bees that keep one from getting to it. For the sake of all beings, I expound the true **Dharma** with skillful means, removing the bees of klesas, revealing the Tathagatagarbha. Endowed with eloquence that knows no obstacle, I preach the **Dharma** of sweet dew, compassionately relieving sentient beings, everywhere helping them to true enlightenment.

Tathagatagarbha Sutra - - - - - - - - It is just like what happens when all the kernels, the husks of which have not yet been washed away, are disdained by someone who is impoverished, and said to be something to be discarded. But although the outside seems like *something useless, the inside is genuine and not to be destroyed. After the husks are removed, it becomes food fit for a king. I see that all kinds of beings have a buddhagarbha hidden by klesas. I preach the removal of those things to enable them to attain universal wisdom. Just as I have a Tathagata nature, so do all beings. When they develop it and purify it, they quickly attain the highest path.*

*Tathagatagarbha Sutra - - - - - - - - It is just like what happens when gold is submerged in impure waste, where no one can see it. But someone with supernatural vision sees it and tells people about it, saying, 'If you get it out and wash it clean, you may do with it as you will,' which causes their relatives and family all to rejoice. The Well-departed One's vision is like this. He sees that for all kinds of beings, the Tathagata nature is not destroyed, though it is submerged in the muddy silt of klesas. So he appropriately expounds the **Dharma** and enables them to manage all things, so that the klesas covering the Buddha nature are quickly removed and beings are purified.*

Tathagatagarbha Sutra - - - - - - - - It is like a great foundry with countless golden statues. Foolish people look at the outside and see only the darkened earthen molds. The master foundry man estimates that they have cooled, and opens them to extract their contents. All impurity is removed and the features clearly revealed. With my Buddha vision I see that all sentient beings are like this. Within the mud shell of passions, all have the Tathagata-nature. By means of adamantine wisdom, we break the mold of the klesas and reveal the Tathagatagarbha, like pure, shining gold. Just as I have seen this and so instructed all the bodhisattvas, so should you accept it, and convert in turn all other beings.

Tathagatagarbha Sutra - - - - - - - - It is like a store of treasure inside the house of an impoverished man. The owner is not aware of it, nor can the treasure speak. For a very long time it is buried in darkness, as there is no one who can tell of its presence. When you have treasure but do not know of it, this causes poverty and suffering. When the Buddha eye observes sentient beings, it sees that, although they transmigrate through the five realms of reincarnation, there is a great treasure in their bodies that is eternal and unchanging. When he sees this, the Buddha teaches on behalf of all beings, enabling them to attain the treasure-store of wisdom, and the great wealth of widely caring for one another. If you believe what I have taught you about all having a treasure store, and practice it faithfully and ardently, employing skillful means, you will quickly attain the highest path.

The exhaustive use of parables in the Mahayana Buddhist texts which date to around the same time as the formation of Christianity opens us up to speculation to just how connected Buddhist missionaries were to the original composers of the Gospel stories and the teachings attributed to Jesus.

Simon

The Jews had been forming what modern news would call "terrorist" groups throughout the Roman Empire. From 115 to 117, Jewish rebels would attack Roman soldiers and citizens in Egypt, Cyrenaica, and Cyprus. The attacks were not just about political rule. Lukuas led the rebels in Cyrenaica. They destroyed temples devoted to Isis, Zeus (Jupiter), Hecate (Trivia), Apollo, Artemis (Diana). Destroying people and cultural symbols of Romans and Greeks and Egyptians was done with religious zeal at eliminating from the world everything that offended their xenophobia. Lukuas sets fire to Alexandria, Egypt, destroying temples. Fifteen years later, Simon bar Kokhba would be inspired to continue their tradition and take it to its logical conclusion: recapture Jerusalem from the Romans and form a united front that would free all of the land of Israel, cleansed and purified of all of this imposed foreign influence and corruption.

Faith. Faith in the Messianic Age. Faith in the Chosen People. Faith in the Promised Land. Faith that God was on their side. Silver coins were made to replace the pagan Roman money, declaring it to be year one, with symbols of angel trumpets and a star of hope. The text on the coins read: **To the freedom of Jerusalem. To the freedom of Israel.** From 132 to 135 the faithful fought on, with faith in the Messiah Simon, with faith in God being on their side. The Jews following Simon were against the Roman Empire ruling their land, against Hellenistic religion and philosophies corrupting their religious purity. All the faithful were called to support the revolution. Even children were taught to fight the Roman soldiers. Any who refused to join were punished.

An interesting window into this is the tradition from Eusebius, and possibly back to Justin Martyr, is that the Jews who refused to support Simon as Messiah were "Christians". Christianity in the period of 132 to 135 was noted as being an alternative to the battles of the failed revolutionaries. This is what makes the Jesus story so unique. Simon played the perfect role as being a Messiah figure. Jesus, as we will see, is an antidote for that way of thinking, a cure for Messianic crusades to rule the world in the name of being the Chosen People of the only true religious tradition on the planet.

It was soon after this that Hadrian became Roman emperor, the emperor that would defeat Simon: Publius Aelius Hadrianus. His empire spanned from Britannia to Africa. He wanted to gather the best from every religious tradition and combine the ideas into a coherent whole: one cosmopolitan pool of ideas shared by all the diversity of the Roman Empire, the best of all combined and assimilated into one enlightened age. The Samaritans had begun to integrate their rites with Greek ideas, their God of Mount Gerizim being equated with Zeus. In Jerusalem, Hadrian decided to build temples to Zeus (Jupiter) and Aphrodite (Venus). The Jews would not integrate into his unified cosmopolitan spirituality.

This is the birth situation for Christianity, for the Jesus story, for the "kingdom not of this world" alternative. By the year 135, over half a million Jewish rebels had died and over a thousand Jewish towns were completely destroyed. Judaea was renamed Syria Palaestina (Palestine) in memory of the Philistines, the original inhabitants, who had lost their land to the tradition of the area being the Promised Land for the Chosen People. After Aelius Hadrianus defeated Simon, he renamed Jerusalem "Aelia Capitolina" after himself, devoting it to Zeus (Jupiter). Jews were forbidden to come close enough to see what once was their Jerusalem. Hadrian banned Judaism from the Roman Empire, repealed after his death in 138. All of this to point out the gravity of to what extreme the Messianic hopes had failed those who put their lives on the line to bet that God would respond to their faith and be on their side.

Where? The Promised Land. Who? The Chosen People. How? The Messiah, the Christ. When? Faith in Prophecy.

Daniel 9:24 Seventy weeks are determined upon thy people and upon thy holy city, to finish the transgression, and to make an end of sins, and to make reconciliation for iniquity, and to bring in everlasting righteousness, and to seal up the vision and prophecy, and to anoint the most Holy.

Seventy years, if the word weeks is interpreted as years, from the destruction of the Temple in the year 70 would be the year 140. In the year 132, when Simon bar Kokhba set himself up as the Nasi (ruling prince) of his renewed Israel, declaring it to be year one, this was getting really close to time. In a working with "prophecy" mindset, 140 stood exactly a week (7 years away) from 133, only a short window of time after Simon was set in place. The timing was critical for the prophecy to be taken seriously. Maybe some of you remember the year changed from 1999 to 2000 when some were convinced that Jesus was going to return and end the world. Fundamentalist mindset is consistent throughout the centuries.

Numbers 24:17-19 I shall see him, but not now: I shall behold him, but not nigh: there shall come a Star out of Jacob, and a Sceptre shall rise out of Israel, and shall smite the corners of Moab, and shall destroy all the children of Sheth. And Edom shall be a possession, Seir also shall be a possession for his enemies; and Israel shall do valiantly. Out of Jacob shall come he that shall have dominion, and shall destroy him that remaineth of the city.

*Rabbi Akiva, the leading Jewish authority on the meaning of the scriptures in the year 132, declared Simon to be "bar Kokhba", to be the Star Child prophesized, the Messiah, the Christ. What does this mean? The official policy of the Jewish leaders backed Simon with an all-out war effort against the Romans. The spirit of the Kitos War continued, but this time it was brought home to Jerusalem. This Jewish uprising was anti-Roman and anti-Hellenism and presented as mandatory in patriotism and faith to the Jewish tradition. Those who refused to join the resistance movement were attacked. The prophecy of the Star smiting, possessing, fighting valiantly, taking dominion, and destroying all foreigners who remained in the city, when put into play, became a very serious movement. They believed in this so strongly that in the end over half a million Jews died and over a thousand of their towns were completely destroyed. Emperor Hadrian is known for ending wars and negotiating peace treaties. The Jews supporting Simon would not give up their faith and determination. Their **Christianity** meant more to them than their lives and they would gladly martyr themselves for God, for Israel, for Jerusalem, and for their Christ, Simon the Star.*

An interesting window into this is mentioned by Eusebius that those who refused to join with Simon were the people who are the ancestors of his form of Christianity. Who planted such a seed in faithful Jewish minds to have them rebel against the resistance movement, to abandon the Messiah? How do you even form an antidote to such poisoned minds? How do you promote a holy city where peace reigns and hatred has no home, whose King rules with wisdom and compassion, a city that is open for all, a city that lives within our hearts? Can such poetic words be mightier than swords?

Faith in God. Faith in tradition, in prophecy, in the agreed upon set of truths. Chosen people of the one and only true god belong in the promised land, destined to rule without any possible foreign force out there to say any differently. Messiah to appear to ensure this dream becomes reality, backed by legions of angels descending from the clouds blowing trumpets and evoking fear and respect. If you have strong enough faith, you don't ask "if" and you don't even ask "when", you just begin as if it is the predestined will of God and know without a doubt that God will provide.

The Kitos War, years 115 to 117, was not fought in the Holy Land, not in Jerusalem. They rallied recognition for the rebel alliance that believed God would provide a hero, a Messiah, a Christ as the Greeks would say, to end the rule of the Roman Empire and make Israel great again. In Alexandria and Cyrene, the terrorists attacked Romans, soldiers and citizens, destroying temples and symbols of Roman and Hellenistic culture, setting fires. The new Caesar, Emperor Hadrian, had just taken control of the Roman legions and, first by words and then by force, set out to hold back the hand of Messianic Judaism.

Those weird references to the Romans "persecuting" the Christians and blaming them for starting fires and causing problems, I was always taught was that the Romans were the bad guys under the influence of Satan who were opposed to the meek mannered early Christian movement and being really mean to them. The Kitos War "Christians" were fire starting terrorists in the name of "Christ", the Greek term for Messiah, the code word for joining the resistance movement to defeat the Roman Empire. What they called Christians in 115 is very different than what we call Christians today. This is the most important thing I've unlearned in the past year of study for this book.

Abomination of Desolation

Vaticinium ex eventu is Latin for hindsight prophecy, making a character speak of an event in the future from the time setting of the character. This makes it sound like prophecy.

Mark 13:14 But when ye shall see the abomination of desolation, spoken of by Daniel the prophet, standing where it ought not, (let him that readeth understand,) then let them that be in Judaea flee to the mountains:

Matthew 24:15-16 When ye therefore shall see the abomination of desolation, spoken of by Daniel the prophet, stand in the holy place, (whoso readeth, let him understand:) Then let them which be in Judaea flee into the mountains:

Luke 21:20-22 And when ye shall see Jerusalem compassed with armies, then know that the desolation thereof is nigh. Then let them which are in Judaea flee to the mountains; and let them which are in the midst of it depart out; and let not them that are in the countries enter thereinto. For these be the days of vengeance, that all things which are written may be fulfilled.

Luke 21:24 And they shall fall by the edge of the sword, and shall be led away captive into all nations: and Jerusalem shall be trodden down of the Gentiles, until the times of the Gentiles be fulfilled.

Matthew and Mark and Luke are "synoptic" which means they are similar and all derived from the same original text. The official story is that Jesus is speaking this prophecy in the year 30, 40 years before the Jerusalem Temple was destroyed during the first Jewish-Roman war.

The city taken, the people exiled and forbidden to return to Jerusalem, describes the situation in 135 after Hadrian takes control of the city and renames it Aelia Capitolina, setting up a statue of Zeus (Jupiter) in the ruins of the Temple grounds (the abomination of desolation, let the reader understand). The end result of the Titus campaign in 70 did not result in the total loss of Jerusalem to the Romans as did the events of 135 with the defeat of Simon bar Kokhba and his high priest, Elazar (Lazarus).

So, what does this mean? The proto-gospel from which Matthew and Mark and Luke, the synoptic gospels, are derived would be dated after the events of the year 135 unless we are to have blind faith that the speaker or the writer knew in advance what was to come 105 years in the future of when they are supposed to have been prophesized. Could the initial Gospel have been introduced in the second century instead of in the first century? Could the initial Gospel have been introduced as an antidote for Messianic revolution, for the original "Christ-ianity" that rallied around leaders like Simon bar Kokhba, for the pre-rabbinic Judaism that proved itself politically and socially instable?

If this suggests the "when" and we have already examined the "why" then all we have left to contemplate is the "who" of the origin of the Gospel of Jesus Christ, son of man, teacher of peace and love, forgiveness and compassion.

Basilides of Alexandria

When all you know about a person is what can be collected from people who really didn't like that person, and you have to fill in all the missing parts with speculation, it is difficult to know for sure if you have guessed correctly. The Catholic Church made it part of the faithful duty of all its members, all its writers and leaders, to make sure it is understood that the Gnostics were naughty. The official policy which needs to be recited back in good faith for the test is that the Gnostics perverted and corrupted the original Jesus tradition with their heretical ideas and their creative expansions. Basilides was just such a Gnostic heretic.

He is placed in Alexandria from 117 to 138, from the onset of the Kitos War through the aftermath of the defeat of Simon bar Kokhba, during the time of Emperor Hadrian and living in a city which was one of Hadrian's retreats, in a city that was the portal for the Greco-Buddhist exchanges of philosophical thought in the Western world, in a city that is noted for the religious tolerance and syncretism that incubated the birth of Gnostic Christianity, in a city that was home for the largest library of spiritual ideas in the ancient world.

Origen said in his Homilies on Luke that Basilides wrote his own Gospel. What he was implying was that it was a corrupted heresy variation of the earlier canonical accepted approved version. Basilides is also linked with Matthew and had written dozens of books expounding the intricate meanings of that Gospel, all of which were lost. If we consider the popularity of his "church" in Alexandria and how Irenaeus and Hippolytus present him as a heretic enemy of the "true church", we can rest assured that "lost" means that the ancient Roman Catholics found and destroyed any of his works that they knew was attributed to him. So we have Basilides as a major player in the formation and understanding of the Gospel texts. Corrupter or originator?

The ideas that made Basilides a heretic to the later Roman Catholic writers, which they saw as a deviation of some earlier purity, probably point to an earlier way of thinking in the Jesus Movement. I don't want to say "Christianity", because I think that word implied Messianic hope-inspired violence at the time. The few Roman references to Christianity, if not outright forgeries, refer to dangerous violent groups that need to be kept in check. Nero in 54 accuses the Christians, read "Messianic revolutionaries", as being the enemies of humanity, starting fires in Rome and stirring up discontent. The Christians that Domitian had to deal with in 81 sound like Messianic rebels, as do the descriptions of Christians in 112 by Pliny and Trajan. If you look backwards in time from Basilides, Christianity was indeed different and he did indeed change it, but as we shall see, it was needed changes and not heretical corruptions of anything that needed its state preserved.

Hippolytus reports that Basilides proposed a transcendent Nothingness beyond the ability of reason to understand, a Supreme God above all gods, ineffable. He rejected the Jewish religion, its God, its Messianic tradition, and yet, he wrote a Gospel. Let that sink in for a moment. The Catholics were to have the New Testament of the combination of Gospel and Epistle traditions contained in the same Bible as the Old Testament of the Jewish scriptures. Catholic version is Jesus is the Jewish Messiah, representing the Jewish god, twisted into a Mystery School dying-resurrecting god-man story. Gnostic version is Jesus is something beyond normal religion, beyond all the gods including the Jewish god, and was neither a Messiah war hero nor a Mystery School human sacrifice, but was a Teacher for those ready to escape from the limitations of human culture and logic and potential. Basilides had a Jesus that was not supportive of Judaism, had a version (earlier or corrupted, take your pick) of the Gospel of Matthew that he was an expert on, and lived in a time and place ripe with the expansion of Mahayana Buddhist thought. You can judge the tree by its fruits.

The points that the Roman Catholic heresy hunter writers made in attacking Basilides were the same points that they would have made in criticizing the Buddhism of their day. Basilides didn't believe in the resurrection of the body, one of the main points in the Apostle's Creed. One of the first responses of Fundamentalists that I hear when they try to figure out what it means that I am Gnostic is the assertion that Gnostics think the Jewish god is the devil and how that sounds so absurd to them. It is a bit of a misconception, the truth of the matter being beyond their ability to paradigm shift from their acquired way of thinking. Basilides was criticized for not believing in hell, but instead speaking of foreign concepts such as metempsychosis (reincarnation) and being spiritually trapped, the reality of karma, and what he called the appendages of the passions holding back the soul to greater potentials. Basilides spoke of salvation as being disentanglement, not as something that can be added to any of us, but rather a discovery of what is already there within each of us, part of our natural makeup. Some people "get it" easily, are predestined to be among the chosen few who take that alternative path, the Gnostics. Most people, though they have it so obviously within themselves, live their lives in ignorance, being driven by the appendages, the collected baggage of desires and fears and reactions and prejudiced conclusions. A lot of people in Alexandria thought Basilides was onto something. His influence lasted for centuries in Alexandria before being crushed out by the Roman Catholic version of Christianity winning out. Winning meant the popes in Rome sent out enough holy thugs that persuaded by fear and destruction that Rome must be right. Might makes right. The meek inherit destruction.

The complete and perfect Understanding is planted in us like a seed which grows upwards and transforms us, evolves us, makes us transcend this mundane world. This "Intermediate Spirit" is what is given to us from the Son who descends from the Nothingness. Gnosticism is so difficult to understand by those who have been programmed by modern Christianity. It is because the origins of Christianity have been erased and replaced with fabrications that make the truths seem like heresies and the fairy tale creations seem like histories. Once you see it, you can't unsee it. The Holy Ghost is given to us from the Son who comes from the Father. The Sacred **Dharma** is given to us from the Buddha who comes from Nirvana. The real "Chosen People" are those who can keep this sacred flame alive, this sacred pool filled, the church, the sangha. The three sonships of Basilides align with the Three Gems of Buddhism: the Buddha, the **Dharma**, and the Sangha. Gospel writer with Buddhist ideas.

When you arrive at such a pure set of ideas, cosmic (universal), transcending cultures and ages, able to be stated in any language with any story characters adapted to local customs, this **Dharma** means more than any previously considered religion or philosophy. It doesn't argue against them; it just makes them no longer matter. It wasn't that Basilides was anti-Semitic, against the Jewish god and religion, it was that he had found truths that propelled him beyond all that. Join Simon in Jerusalem to defeat the Romans? Support an *ancient concept of a tribal god who insisted there should be no other gods before him and the world should be purified of every trace of other religions? Support the destruction of temples and libraries and art and literature in the name of making Judaism great again? Was Basilides in Alexandria, at the onset of the latest war to end all wars, against the Jewish god as being the focal point of a lot of violent evil taking place? I think so. He was against the "Christians", the violence supporting Simon. Simon? Nail this idiot to a Roman cross already!*

And now for something completely different...

Gospel, good news, alternative to the only way that they are able to see it, talk about it, represent it. Different values, different goals. The antidote for the recent epidemic of poisoned minds.

Lotus Sutra 14 - - - - - - - - This Lotus Sutra contains attainable understandable wisdom for sentient beings. **In the face of the great amount of hostility in the world**, it is difficult to accept. It has not been preached before my preaching of it now. It is the **secret treasure of the Buddhas**.

Satipatthanasamyutta 31 - - - - - - - - In regard to **things unheard before**, there arose in me vision, knowledge, wisdom, **Gnosis**, and light.

Payasi Sutta 11 - - - - - - - - The other realm cannot be seen with the physical eyes. You must clarify the divine eye.

Tao Te Ching 14 - - - - - - - - **That which eyes have not seen**, ear has not heard, mind has not contemplated, senses cannot detect, and intellect cannot rationalize, can be realized in meditation.

Thomas 17 Jesus said, "I will give you what no eye has seen, what no ear has heard, what no hand has touched, what has not arisen in the human heart."

The original Jesus, the Joshua of the Bible, was the leader of the Chosen People across the Jordan River into the Promised Land. He did so with an army and a great deal of violence. That land which you have never seen, promised to Moses, Joshua (Jesus) will give to you if you follow him. The idea was for the new Joshua (Jesus) to lead the new special people across the new obstacle into the new homeland, that not of this world. Buddha named the process of awakening as crossing the stream. Who is this new leader showing the narrow way that leads to the new promised land? The idea of there being the Mysteries, the secrets for the initiated, the **Gnosis** that once understood gives you the keys to advancing to a new reality, was ripe in the Greek speaking world at the time Christianity was forming.

Crossing over a Jordan that's hard to define, hard to know, but some can feel it. This promised land beyond is not of this dimension. Anyone can cross over, but you have to ready yourself for the experience, and be willing to evolve in a way that will never allow *you to think the same way again. Crossing over means leaving behind that which cannot cross with you.*

*Tao Te Ching 09 - - - - - - - - The buildup of wealth and position is the seed for destruction. If you have merit and fame you should **abandon it**. This is the Way of Heaven.*

Thomas 110 Jesus said, "Let one who has found the world, and has become wealthy, renounce the world."

Who is going to own Jerusalem? Who is going to control the city and everything in it? The Nasi Simon sits on his throne for his brief moment of success and rule. If you win, you should consider losing. The first shall be last. If Simon had have won his revolutionary war against Hadrian and his Roman legions, he would have been the first pope of Jerusalem. He basically wanted a world where organized religion was powerful enough to control the world around its center. Like the Holy Roman Empire was to become in Europe, what if there had have become a Holy Jewish Empire in the Middle East? Every build up success of a political area drawn on a map ends up being obsoleted by future success stories of distant Barbarians whose gods have promised them their own victories and their armies fight with their own faith and stubborn devotion. There is no good revolution, just power changing hands.

Resonance

There can be found references in Jewish scriptures to a few aspects of the life of Jesus and his teachings, mined out by redactors of the Gospel story in good faith that Jesus was indeed the fulfilment of prophecies, the completion of Law, the refection of all that is good in Jewish tradition. But Jesus is not quoting from Proverbs, not singing Psalms, and not validating those who want to label him as Messiah King or son of David. The Jesus of the Gospel is not yet the Suffering Servant personification of Isaiah, not yet the only son of God incarnate, not yet wrapped up with all of the Christology and dogmatic assertions that would grow in centuries to come and define the Roman Catholic Christian faith of who Jesus is and what he stands for and what that all means.

*From the Virgin Birth through the Ascension there are parallels, resonances, detail points, that make the story of Jesus like the story of Siddhartha Gautama, the tales of the Buddha popular in the Greco-Buddhism worldview. Not just a few parallels. If you take just the Sermon on the Mount alone, there is so much more in common with Buddhist and Taoist writings than any parallels that could be found in Jewish writings. Instead of these being thought to be a New Testament to append onto the Old Testament of Jewish writings, it would be more accurate to consider these to be a new Vehicle for the Greco-Buddhist **Dharma**. St. Clement of Alexandria knew of Buddha and mentioned him in his Stromatateis, written in the year 202. Clement believed that there is Universal Wisdom. He adopted a liberal interpretation of scriptures, seeing teaching allegories instead of literal truths, and understanding relationships of ideas with other spiritual traditions and philosophies such as that of Plato. His collection of Christian ideas included those of the Gnostics, ideas that were to be later repressed and forgotten.*

This window of understanding was to close, the world of mystics like Clement buried under creeds and councils. Dogmatic assertion becoming more important than freshly inspired insight. The popes in Rome were to have their hands full in suppressing heretical thoughts for centuries. Many of these powerful forbidden ideas originated in Alexandria. Free thinking was seen as the Evil that was defiling the one holy Catholic and Apostolic faith. The Pachomian monastics maintain a library and a book binding operation. 67 miles away during the time the Nag Hammadi Library was buried, a collection of 52 tractates of early Christian thought. The connection of the monastics to the Gnostic library can only be speculation. The very idea of there being Christian monks and nuns, holy orders of people devoted to spiritual pursuits, links back to there being Buddhist monks and nuns. Prayer beads and incense and silent meditation. The Gnostic values of leaving the world and searching for God may have found a home in the heart of some of the followers of St. Pachomius. These texts were hidden from the destructive hands of the Church Police around the year 350, and just in time. In 391, faithful Christians stormed the Great Library of Alexandria and destroyed all of the books, centuries of collections of the best ideas from around the known world. You can imagine the faithful with their idolized "no other books before me" Bible in one hand and a torch in the other. In 415, faithful Christians attacked Hypatia of Alexandria, a woman who was one of the wisest Neo-Platonic philosophers, killing her and persecuting her disciples. We should consider the "onward Christian soldiers" mindset of what was to become Christianity and how this relates back to the original dream and vision of those who set to ink the first Jesus traditions with the hopes that they may inspire change for a better world.

The resonances, the parallels of thought, each individual one could be explained away, but gather them all and zoom out to the whole collection, to the holistic set of archetypical patterns etched into place, and a story that cannot be dismissed becomes revealed. Different and yet the same, like gardens composed of different types of flowers that are laid out in the same arrangement of patterns.

Giving birth to the Buddha

What does the word "Buddha" mean? Awakened, blossoming with new hope. Something new? Something completely different. When everything is going wrong, people look for any sign of hope, any symbol of change, any wind blowing in a new direction. Simon bar Kokhba played on this human nature response by preaching that he could make Jerusalem great again, that he is the Christ Star that has appeared in the darkened skies of Roman oppression, the son of God. Change can inspire faith and hope. Everyone couldn't have bought in to the violent acts of terrorism, hiding in wait in underground tunnels. Everyone couldn't have felt that strongly that the Romans were the problem and Greek philosophy was the Devil trying to corrupt the faithful. Something else new? The Kitos War didn't work and it was obvious that Hadrian would send in as many legions of highly trained Roman soldiers with catapults and strategies learned from encounters with situations from there to Britain. The "Christians", the Messianic revolutionaries, the Simon supporters, didn't have a prayer of a chance.

What if an alternative was conceived, a holy child that didn't inherit the need to support the tradition and culture and heritage of his father? He wasn't son of God, not the child of some divine lineage of some ancient fabled King David of Camelot. He was son of humanity. What if this child grew up without supporting the xenophobia and conflict, didn't speak out of that collection of ideas, didn't promote antiquated religious practices and attitudes? What if this child grew into a Teacher who could give an alternative to being "Christian", to being a Messianic revolutionary, to supporting people like Simon? An alternative to Christ, an exit door, a narrow way that led away from the joining in with all of the destruction and tension and hate and fear! What the world needed was a hero, not of military ability, but rather of a working knowledge of change through the application of peace and love and unity. Listen and you can hear the baby crying over the sounds of yet another terrorist attack.

Born Again

Itivuttaka 4:1 - - - - - - - - You are my children, born of **Dharma**, *created by* **Dharma**, *born of the Spirit and not of the flesh.*

John 1:12-13 But as many as received him, to them gave he power to become the sons of God, even to them that believe on his name: Which were born, not of blood, nor of the will of the flesh, nor of the will of man, but of God.

Born again is a Buddhist concept. Born of the Spirit as contrasted with being physically born is a Buddhist concept. Not a Jewish concept.

New family, not defined by race or religion or politics or wealth, but of siblings of **Dharma**, *of* **Gnosis**, *of shared "born again" experience. It is a family that is cosmopolitan (universal), catholic (all inclusive), timeless, ecumenical (transcending differences), a heart set (like mind set, but of emotion) of resonance with compassion, with empathy, with peace, with celebrating diversities and embracing differences. One world family. Children of Jesus. Children of Buddha. Not the sons of the Chosen People as exclusive to the rest of the world, but the sons of man, the children of humanity, the inclusive family of us all.*

Samanamandika Sutta 08 - - - - - - - - You who have arrived at the state in which you do no evil bodily actions, utter no evil speech, have no evil intentions, and do not make money at any evil livelihood—I describe as being like a young tender newborn lying infant.

John 3:3 Jesus answered and said unto him, Verily, verily, I say unto thee, Except a man be born again, he cannot see the kingdom of God.

Kingdom of God. Dharma of Nirvana. Initiated Membership in something beyond the limitations of how people around you think and act.

Vimalakirti Nirdesa Sutra 2 - - - - - - - - Friends, the body of a Tathagata is the body of **Dharma**, *born of* **Gnosis**. *The body of a Tathagata is born of the stores of merit and wisdom. It is born of morality, of meditation, of wisdom, of the liberations, and of the knowledge and vision of liberation. It is born of love, compassion, joy, and impartiality. It is born of charity, discipline, and self-control. It is* *born of the path of ten virtues. It is born of patience and gentleness. It is born of the roots of virtue planted by solid efforts. It is born of the concentrations, the liberations, the meditations, and the absorptions. It is born of learning, wisdom, and liberative technique. It is born of the thirty-seven aids to enlightenment. It is born of mental quiescence and transcendental analysis. It is born of the ten powers, the four fearlessnesses, and the eighteen special qualities. It is born of all the transcendences. It is born from sciences and superknowledges. It is born of the abandonment of all evil qualities, and of the collection of all good qualities. It is born of truth. It is born of reality. It is born of conscious awareness. "Friends, the body of a Tathagata is born of innumerable good works. Toward such a body you should turn your aspirations, and, in order to eliminate the sicknesses of the passions of all living beings, you should conceive the spirit of unexcelled, perfect enlightenment."*

John 3:7 Marvel not that I said unto thee, Ye must be born again.

*To give birth to yourself is an interesting concept. You didn't select your parents, who your mother embraced as your father to conceive of you. Spiritually, you are your own mother, you embrace the Buddha and become impregnated with the **Dharma** and give birth to your understanding (**Gnosis**) of your true nature.*

Reborn is repurposed, renewed, recycled, re-directed. You are no longer one of them, no longer signed up for their battles, no longer have membership in their religion. You have seen a better way, a wiser way, a way of wisdom, compassion, openness, patience, peacefulness, fearlessness in standing up against the common way. It is a rebirth in abandoning the old and collecting the new, waking up to a new reality, a new focus of consciousness.

Mother acquires a virtuous nature

The serene holy mother holding the sacred child of hope was a known spiritual image in Alexandria. Long before the Mother Mary and Baby Jesus statues swept across Europe, the same statues were understood to be Mother Isis and Baby Horus. Lady Wisdom has a Child, full of knowledge, meek and mild, he will teach the world to know the power of his Mother's Love.

*Mahapadana Sutta 1:17-19; Acchariya-Abbhuta Sutta 08-10 - - - - - - - - When a Bodhisattva has entered his mother's womb, four divas (angels, gods) come to protect him from the four quarters. Let no man, no non-human, no one whatsoever harm this Bodhisattva or this Bodhisattva's mother. **His mother acquires a virtuous nature**. She has no sensual thoughts concerning a man and she cannot be overcome by any man with lustful thoughts.*

Matthew 1:18 Now the birth of Jesus Christ was on this wise: When as his mother Mary was espoused to Joseph, before they came together, she was found with child of the Holy Ghost.

Luke 1:34-35 Then said Mary unto the angel, How shall this be, seeing I know not a man? And the angel answered and said unto her, The Holy Ghost shall come upon thee, and the power of the Highest shall overshadow thee: therefore also that holy thing which shall be born of thee shall be called the Son of God.

Before the Answer can be born, the mother of the Answer has to be pure, protected, devoted, prepared. Make the mother virtuous enough. But who is this mother? The stories about the mothers of Siddhartha and of Jesus could be taken as historical accounts, articles of faith, objects of devotion. What if the stories are parables? What if each of us is the mother of the Answer? What if we purify and protect ourselves from worldly influences enough for us to conceive of the Answer and give it birth and life and prepare it a home?

In a world of conflict, patriotism is held up as a faith, support the fathers, the patriarchal network of belonging. What if the answer is to have no father to have to fight and die for? Break the chain!

The story of Mara on the surface poses quite the literal Zoroastrian style battle between good and evil. Mara is a demon that tries to keep Gautama from taking his role as Buddha. Mara is adept in violence and waves of pleasures and doubts that are used to distract Gautama. He is the tempter, the allure of the mundane values of the world out there. Mara leads an army playing on the field of life and death.

Mara can be interpreted as the collection of internal vices and attachments that keep us from enlightenment, a manifestation of deluded thoughts, a personification of the human ego run amok. Mara reverberates in our consciousness with impulses of rage and intention of violence, of lust and desire, greed and pride. Mara is only as strong as we allow and can be overcome by anyone who can tame the beast demon within.

It is from the Mara mind that the Buddha is first conceived. The first thought that there could be a better way, of peace and love, of divergent harmony, of cosmopolitan truth overshadowing xenophobic differences. The desire to Know what it would be like if the world were a different place, the loosening of the grip on the selfish goals of the world out there, allows for this internal Buddha to form in the mind, the Seed to be planted, the Fountain to be turned on, the Light to be fueled.

In this way, we each are Mara and we each are Buddha. We get to decide which road we choose to walk down. Mara will get plenty of support and encouragement from the world out there. Buddha will have to be protected and nurtured, kept away from the poisons and fed with the spiritual vitamins.

When words from different traditions sound the same, we can consider if they are related. The name Mara in the Buddhist tradition is similar to the name Mary in the Jesus tradition. What if we read the story about Mary and baby Jesus in the light of our contemplations about Mara and Siddhartha? Mary is the child of the war god Mars, the inheritor of all of the conflict and hate and fear of her people, the daughter of the Temple of the old religion that is generating so much suffering.

In this light, the Mary that conceives of Jesus without any outside influence whatsoever is a parable for each of us who have taken that first step towards Enlightenment. The Child within us is our newfound meditative state of absorption, our newly acquired Thought applied to our lives. The Child is the new us being born from within the context of our former lives. The Child is the first key to it all, thus the importance of Christmas, of the celebration of the Baby who will *be the Answer to all our Enlightenment needs, of the beginning of a new year.*

Awakening the Child

Acchariya-Abbhuta Sutta 16 - - - - - - - *Ananda—When the Bodhisattva came forth from this mother's womb, first gods received him, then people.*

Sutta Nipata 686-688 - - - - - - - - **The newborn prince was shining**, *glowing, beautiful, like fresh gold coming out of the furnace by the master goldsmith. To see the prince was to see a glow, a glow of a fire,* **like all of the stars together of the night sky**, *the intensity of an autumn sun shining on a clear blue day. This sight filled the hermit with great joy. He delighted in the skies above his head, with transparent beings holding up an endless canopy with a thousand spokes holding up the center. Countless gods waved fans made of gold.*

Acchariya-Abbhuta Sutta 07; 21 - - - - - - - - *When the Bodhisattva passed away from the Tusita Heaven and descended into his mother's womb, then an immeasurable light surpassing the splendor of the gods appeared in the world. Even in those abysmal world interspaces of vacancy,* **gloom, and utter darkness**, *where the moon and the sun, mighty and powerful as they are, cannot make light prevail—there too a great immeasurable light surpassing the splendor of the gods appeared.*

Sadharmapundarika Sutra 7; Lotus Sutra 07 - - - - - - - *The dark distant land, which never saw the light of the sun or the light of the moon, glowed with a bright light [...] Our homes have a glow that was never before known. Why is this? We all want to know. It is because of the birth of a very virtuous divine being—a Buddha appearing in the world. That could be the only explanation for this bright light shining all around, high and low. [...]* **We have never seen such a sign before, with the common quest to travel through countless lands together to reach the origin of this light**. *The Buddha has appeared in the world to save sentient beings from their suffering. [...] The time will come when* **I will be a Buddha in another land and will be known by a different name**.

Tathagatagarbha Sutra - - - - - - - - *It is like* **an impoverished woman whose appearance is common and vile**, *but who bears a son of noble degree who will become a universal monarch. Replete with seven treasures and all virtues, he will possess as king the four* quarters of the earth. But she is incapable of knowing this and conceives only thoughts of inferiority. I see that all beings are like infants in distress. **Within their bodies is the Tathagatagarbha, but they do not realize it.** So I tell bodhisattvas, 'Be careful not to consider yourselves inferior. Your bodies are Tathagatagarbhas; they always contain the light of the world's salvation.' If you exert yourselves and do not spend a lot of time sitting in the meditation hall, **you will attain the path of very highest realization and save limitless beings**.

Salvation is the meaning of the name Jesus. The "world's salvation" is contrasted with the idea of a hero savior for one specific people. There was great talk and hopes and expectations for a Jewish Messiah to appear to save the Jewish people from Roman rule. To take the Greek word for Messiah, Christ, and combine it with the name meaning salvation, "Jesus Christ" is to be born as a cosmopolitan Answer, a hero on the side of everyone on the planet, the end of xenophobic conflict and destruction, the Christmas child of peace in a war torn world.

Matthew 2:2 Saying, Where is he that is born King of the Jews? for we have seen his star in the east, and are come to worship him.

Luke 1:78 Through the tender mercy of our God; whereby the dayspring from on high hath visited us,

Child arrives

Sutta Nipata 689-691 - - - - - - - - **The long-haired holy man gazed at the child, holding him with great joy**. *The Buddha was being held by a man who had waited for his coming, who knew the appearance of his arrival, who filled with great joy did speak loudly these words—Without compare, this is the absolute perfect person. Remembering his old age and soon coming death, the holy man began to cry in his sadness.*

Luke 2:25-29 And, behold, there was a man in Jerusalem, whose name was Simeon; and the same man was just and devout, waiting for the consolation of Israel: and the Holy Ghost was upon him. And it was revealed unto him by the Holy Ghost, that he should not see death, before he had seen the Lord's Christ. And he came by the Spirit into the temple: and when the parents brought in the child Jesus, to do for him after the custom of the law, Then took he him up in his arms, and blessed God, and said, Lord, now lettest thou thy servant depart in peace, according to thy word:

The old age sees the dawning of the new age. The old order is rapidly fading and failing, suffering in the pains of antiquated ideas and waves of violent protest at the need to morph into something new and different. The child is the symbol for renewal, the Christmas baby giving hope for a better new year to come. Searching for consolation, for peace. The child was not to grow to be the warrior Messiah Nasi. What he was come to bring, to offer, was a transformation well needed and long overdue, a reformation.

What if Simon had a do over? What if instead of taking matters into his own hands and creating so much violence and destruction he had have embraced the consolation Child and walked away an old man at peace? The pen can dream of variations that the sword can never understand.

Sutta Nipata 693 - - - - - - - - *This prince will discover the fulfillment of absolute enlightenment.* **The holy way of life** *will become clearly understood.*

Luke 2:40 And the child grew, and waxed strong in spirit, filled with wisdom: and the grace of God was upon him.

Potential must be lived out if it is to have any true value and meaning. In the Buddha story, Prince Siddhartha Gautama had to get out and live the holy life. In the Jesus story, Jesus had to wander the villages and wildernesses. Each had to grow, discover, strengthen, live and understand, collecting wisdom and grace and focus, even though they were mystically born into the assignments.

Cleaning house

Lotus Sutra 06 - - - - - - - - **His realm will be decorated for his majesty, cleansed of impurities and evils**, *discarded trash, overgrown thorns, and disgusting waste. The land will be made smooth without hills or valleys, without pits or protrusions.*

Matthew 3:3 For this is he that was spoken of by the prophet Esaias, saying, The voice of one crying in the wilderness, Prepare ye the way of the Lord, make his paths straight.

"Preparing the way" is quoted from "Second" Isaiah, the Messianic hope that God is powerful enough to send a Leader that will make Israel great again, a reference to the "messiah" Cyrus, the anointed chosen one to rebuild and restore and protect the Chosen People. It is a loaded quote to present in the light of Simon bar Kokhba's rebellion in the year 132. He convinced a lot of Jews to rebel against Roman occupation and proclaimed himself Nasi (prince) ruler of the new Jerusalem. The respected Rabbi Akiva declared Simon to be the Messiah, the promised star of hope to light the way.

It is obvious how to prepare for war, spread the propaganda of hatred for those who are different and form a united front against a common enemy. Question in the context of the "Jesus" story: how to prepare for peace? What ways of thinking have to be turned on their heads? What fears and prejudices have to be thrown out? What narrow mindedness has to be swept away? What all needs to change to prepare the way for the Prince of Peace to rule in a world of conflicts and divisions? Can the pen be mightier than the sword? You bet you.

Cut them off at the root

Nalakapana Sutta 7 - - - - - - - - Abandon the defilements that keep you coming back, that give you only trouble, fruits ripening in suffering, coming back to grow old and die. **Cut them off at the root**, *leave them as a dying stump, left behind and unable to regrow.*

Matthew 3:10 And now also the axe is laid unto the root of the trees: therefore every tree which bringeth not forth good fruit is hewn down, and cast into the fire.

If you are in charge of an orchard of fruit trees, you take care of the trees that you get good fruit from and cut down the trees that you don't get good fruit from. You wouldn't have to have this explained to you. The orchard is symbolic of the mind.

Donald in Mathmagic Land 1959: "Uh-oh. Look at the condition of your mind: antiquated ideas! Bungling! False concepts! Superstitions! Confusion! To think straight, we'll have to clean house."

What has to be cut off, left behind, forgotten, left empty and abandoned? Now in the context of the war Simon was demanding, those who would not join must die, the traitors, the unpatriotic, the unfaithful. John the Baptist is sitting in as a foil for Simon in the Gospel story, a leader of the old order, the old way of thinking, the old goals and plans and dreams. Turn the page, flip the coin, and with Jesus what has to be cut off, left behind, forgotten, left empty and abandoned? Preparation is different. What is standing in the way is different.

Get rid of what doesn't work

*Kakacupama Sutta 08 - - - - - - - - A large tree grove was choked with weeds. It was tended by a man who cared for it. He cut down and threw out the crooked saplings throughout, **cleaning the grove** and tending to the straight and well-formed saplings. The grove will now come to growth, increase, and fulfillment.*

Luke 13:6-9 He spake also this parable; A certain man had a fig tree planted in his vineyard; and he came and sought fruit thereon, and found none. Then said he unto the dresser of his vineyard, Behold, these three years I come seeking fruit on this fig tree, and find none: cut it down; why cumbereth it the ground? And he answering said unto him, Lord, let it alone this year also, till I shall dig about it, and dung it: And if it bear fruit, well: and if not, then after that thou shalt cut it down.

Three years was the duration of Simon's success in taking control of Jerusalem from the Romans, 132 to 135. Hadrian's legions came through Palestine "cleaning the grove" to the tune of completely destroying over a thousand settlements.

Apocalypse of Peter 2:1-6 And ye, receive ye the parable of the fig-tree theron: as soon as its shoots have gone forth and its boughs have sprouted, the end of the world will come." And I, Peter, answered and said unto him, "Explain to me concerning the fig-tree, and how we shall perceive it, for throughout all its days does the fig-tree sprout and every year it brings forth its fruit and for its master. What then meaneth the parable of the fig-tree? We know it not" – And the Master answered and said unto me, "Doest thou not understand that the fig-tree is the house of Israel? Even as a man hath planted a fig-tree in his garden and it brought forth no fruit, and he sought its fruit for many years. When he found it not, he said to the keeper of his garden, 'Uproot the fig-tree that our land may not be unfruitful for us.' And the gardener said to God, 'We thy servants wish to clear it of weeds and to dig the grounds around it and to water it. If it does not then bear fruit, we will immediately remove its roots from the garden and plant another one in its place.' Hast thou not grasped that the fig-tree is the house of Israel? Verily, I say to you, when its boughs have sprouted at the end, then shall deceiving

Christs come, and awaken hope with the words: 'I am Christ, who am now come into the world.'

The "deceiving Christ" was Simon bar Kokhba, for he was supported by the Jewish priesthood and the people who joined him in revolution in the year 132, only to see most of them dead and the rest exiled and forbidden to come within viewing distance of what was once Jerusalem. The Mark text follows the Apocalypse of Peter text, but without the explicit explanation of what the fig tree really stands for. Mark wraps the fig tree story around the cleansing of the temple, creating a completed pericope. The fruitless tree is like the commercialized temple. Matthew makes the withering of the fig tree instant instead of the observing it the following day as in Mark.

Mark 11:12-14 And **on the morrow**, when they were come from Bethany, he was hungry: And seeing a fig tree afar off having leaves, he came, if haply he might find any thing thereon: and when he came to it, he found nothing but leaves; **for the time of figs was not yet.** And Jesus answered and said unto it, No man eat fruit of thee hereafter for ever. And his disciples heard it.

What takes its place is the statement that "this generation shall not pass" which takes away the focus from the 135 timeframe if we are to read the Christ story as events from the first century. The "fig tree" of Pilate had been given enough chances to prove he had any good in him at all. As that was not the case, his legacy was cut down. His reign of terror come to an end. In the context of how this is presented in Luke, this is a reference to, or a prophecy of, Pilate's being taken out of office. This was in the year 36. Second century Christians would have read this in the context of the events of Hadrian defeating Simon bar Kokhba, as the Apocalypse of Peter text hints at. The "three years" of Luke 13:7 would be from year 132 through 135.

Masters of knowledge go to wash

Maha-Assapura Sutta 25 - - - - - - - - A bhikkhu has been washed who has washed off evil unwholesome states that defile.

Brahmanasamyutta 21 - - - - - - - - The Buddha answered—The **Dharma** *is a lake with fords of virtue, a peaceful lake the good recommend to the good. Where the* **masters of knowledge go to wash**, *they come out at the far shore with dry limbs.*

Matthew 3:11 I indeed baptize you with water unto repentance. But he that cometh after me is mightier than I, whose shoes I am not worthy to bear: he shall baptize you with the Holy Ghost, and with fire:

Water is one way to cleanse. The word for ghost is the same as the word for wind. Think of a leaf blower clearing a lawn filled with leaves. Think of a desert wind sandblasting the walls, removing every stain of impurity. Fire is the way to cleanse metals, to burn off impurities. One more parable symbolism at play that is saying the same thing in a different way: wash it away, cut it down, clean up the place for the arrival of the Child. The parable imagery can be played with in many views. Enter into the pool of **Gnosis**. *Pour upon yourself from the cup of overflowing love.*

Voices divine

Akankheyya Sutta 15 - - - - - - - - You who fulfill the precepts may wish to hear the sounds of voices divine and human from near and far.

Matthew 3:17   And lo a voice from heaven, saying, This is my beloved Son, in whom I am well pleased.

Sometimes you hear a different voice, a different drummer, a different song, a different message. Jesus is born and now Jesus is initiated, baptized, confirmed to have fulfilled the precepts, acknowledged to be on the Right Path. Sometimes you need just a word of acknowledgement to prove you are not just losing your mind in this alternative to becoming one more recruit in their holy war of the moment. Perhaps even excommunicated into a solitary life of contemplating your divergent narrow path, it is nice to hear the cosmos throw you a sign. This Child, this Son, you have conceived and given birth to is acknowledged to be of somewhere beyond all this. The Gnostics called the beyond all this the "Pleroma" meaning fullness, while the Buddhists called it "Nirvana" meaning emptiness. This heaven beyond is the source for the voice of affirmation here in the Gospel. No matter what people say, know you are on the right track.

The Material World of Mara

Marasamyutta 18 - - - - - - - *Blessed are those who live on nothing at all. We shall feed on rapture like the streaming radiance devas (angels, gods). Then Mara the Evil One realized the Blessed and Fortunate One knows, and sad and disappointed he disappeared right there.*

Mahasaccaka Sutta 27 - - - - - - - - *Suppose I stop eating food entirely. Then deities came to me saying they will infuse heavenly food into the pores of my skin and I will live on that.*

Matthew 4:3-4 And when the tempter came to him, he said, If thou be the Son of God, command that these stones be made bread. But he answered and said, It is written, Man shall not live by bread alone, but by every word that proceedeth out of the mouth of God.

Being a consumer, thinking about food, what to enjoy, what to stock up on, what to purchase, is a major factor in living in the material world. We all have to eat. We all like eating some things more than other things. Fasting is a spiritual tool in several cultures. Stop the repeated habit of being focused on what's for lunch and consider what else there is out there to live for.

The temptation of Jesus by Satan and the temptation of Siddhartha by Mara are the same stories with different names. Feed your stomachs. Feed your ego. Feed your greed. Or feed your awakening.

Mahaparinibbana Sutta - - - - - - - - *Mara—May the Enlightened One now reign as king, the Perfected One rule with justice. If the Enlightened One spoke to the largest mountain in the Himalayas, the mountain would turn into gold.*

Marasamyutta 20 - - - - - - - - *Mara—If the Blessed One wishes, he need only resolve that the largest of the Himalayan Mountains turn into gold and it would happen. Buddha—How could a person turn to sensual pleasures that has known the source for suffering? Knowing acquisition as bondage in this world, I should rather wish for it to disappear.*

Matthew 4:8-10 Again, the devil taketh him up into an exceeding high mountain, and sheweth him all the kingdoms of the world, and the glory of them; And saith unto him, All these things will I give thee, if thou wilt fall down and worship me. Then saith Jesus unto him, Get thee hence, Satan: for it is written, Thou shalt worship the Lord thy God, and him only shalt thou serve.

Wealth is the next greatest trick of the material world. How much stuff can you afford to accumulate? Bow down to the almighty god of money and play the financial game in the right way and financial success can be yours. Taking a vow of poverty and detachment is a spiritual tool in several cultures. Stop the repeated habit of being focused on what all you possess and consider what else there is out there to live for.

Other Voice

*Mahasakuludayi Sutta 6 - - - - - - - - When the recluse Gautama is teaching the **Dharma** to several hundred followers, at that time there is no sound, not a cough, not a clearing of one throat. All in that large assembly are poised in suspense of the **Dharma** that **the Blessed One then teaches**.*

Matthew 5:1-2 And seeing the multitudes, he went up into a mountain: and when he was set, his disciples came unto him: And he opened his mouth, and taught them, saying,

The Sermon on the Mount is the most concentrated resonance with Buddhism found in the Gospels. It has been compared to the teachings of the Stoics out of the need to explain where the ideas came from. If we think of Jesus as representing the Jewish tradition, then we would expect the Sermon on the Mount to quote from the Psalms and Proverbs and the best ideas from the Prophets and the Jewish Wisdom literature. And while there can be found a few resonances of ideas from that culture, it is nowhere near the synoptic display of parallels to Buddhist and Taoist texts. Buddha, Siddhartha, was mainly a teacher, everything else was secondary to his explaining to others how to achieve his way of thinking and feeling and valuing and identifying. In the Sermon on the Mount, Matthew chapters five through seven, Jesus is presented as the great teacher. No later Christological concepts are considered. Jesus is not preaching "Christianity" here, nor is he an advocate of "Judaism" either. He is the Other Voice, the alternative, the foreign collection of ideas that the xenophobic minds are so afraid will be unleased and allowed to corrupt their purity of tradition. Their fears were justified.

Possess nothing, free from all attachment

Tao Te Ching 03 - - - - - - - - *If the Perfect Sage wishes to convince people to abandon their divisions, he should **not set aside those considered better by praising them**.*

Gandhari Dhammapada 167 - - - - - - - - *Happiness is living **without possessions** among those who possess much. Happiness is living without ties. Happiness is living **without struggling** among those who strive anxiously.*

Sakkasamyutta 14 - - - - - - - - *You who take refuge in the Sangha and develop right views are **truly not poor** for yours is a life not lived in vain.*

Udanavarga 33:52 - - - - - - - - - *He who is **free from all attachment**, he I say is a holy man.*

Tao Te Ching 70 - - - - - - - - *The perfect sage dresses in the cheap clothing of The Poor, but treasures **The Way** like a hidden gem.*

Dhammapada 15:04 - - - - - - - - *To live with the most joy, you must possess nothing. To **live on such joy** is to become like a glowing god.*

Matthew 5:3 Blessed are the poor in spirit: for theirs is the kingdom of heaven.

Prosperity Gospel is a concept that states if you are good with God that you will become rich. The milk and honey of the Promised Land will all be yours. It is more blessed to be poor is not an ancient Jewish value. It is the antithesis of all of the talk of God will bless you. Don't play their games. Don't envy them. Don't aspire to be like them. Your destiny is different.

Demand nothing to go your way

Devaputtasamyutta 18 - - - - - - - - *I wish for you that you remain untroubled and that no reason for delight ever be found in you.* **Delight comes to you who are miserable**. *Misery comes to you who are delighted.*

Khandhasamyutta 76 - - - - - - - - *Having reached **the state of being tamed**, they are victors in the world. The enlightened are supreme in the world.*

Culakammavibhanga Sutta 16 - - - - - - - - *You who are **not obstinate and arrogant**, that respect those worthy of respect, rising up in their presence, offering a seat, making way, with honor, respect, reverence, and veneration, wherever reborn will be honored, respected, reverenced, and venerated.*

Matthew 5:4-5 Blessed are they that mourn: for they shall be comforted. Blessed are the meek: for they shall inherit the earth.

Messiah to come is a concept that states if we all join with the Hero that we will win the battle, cast off the foreign rule, gain control of our own Promised Land, inherit our God-given destiny. It is more blessed to be meek and mournful than brave and arrogant is not an ancient Messianic Jewish value. It is the antithesis of all of that talk of God being on our side if we only we could have strong enough faith. Paradigm shift in thinking, in values, in faith.

Counter-light

Anuruddha Sutta 16 - - - - - - - *Suppose an oil lamp burning with pure oil and a pure wick burned very brightly. So too a bhikkhu abides resolved upon and **pervading a pure radiance**.*

Iddhipadasamyutta 20 - - - - - - - *With a mind that is open and unenveloped, **develop a mind imbued with light**.*

Brahmanasamyutta 09 - - - - - - - - *Give up on tending to fire made of wood. Kindle the inner light, concentrated, eternally blazing, **composed of mind**.*

Lotus Sutra 21 - - - - - - - - *After the One Thus Come has passed into extinction, the person who knows the sutras preached by the Buddha, their meaning and relevance and order, preaching them in truth according to the principles received—this person will be **a light passing through the world**, erasing the darkness, leading countless bodhisattvas (saints) to take refuge in the single Way.*

Vatthupama Sutta 21, Mahavacchagotta Sutta 15 - - - - - - - - *I turn upright that which has been knocked down, **revealing the hidden**, showing the Way to those who were lost, holding a lamp in the darkness so those who had eyes to see could then see.*

Bhikkhusamyutta 7 - - - - - - - - *When the wise man is surrounded by fools, they do not recognize his wisdom if he does not speak. He should **speak and explain** the **Dharma**. He should wave his flag high. Well-spoken words are his flag. The **Dharma** is the flag of those who see.*

Matthew 5:14-16 Ye are the light of the world. A city that is set on an hill cannot be hid. Neither do men light a candle, and put it under a bushel, but on a candlestick; and it giveth light unto all that are in the house. Let your light so shine before men, that they may see your good works, and glorify your Father which is in heaven.

The world is run by the fools. Sometimes they force their way in as kings and royalty. Sometimes they are voted in because enough people resonated with their campaign speech. Then they play with governing the realm of money and mind control and war and structuring society. They play with laws and media and education and propagating divisions and xenophobic fears. The lights of change come from faint candles of individuals who see beyond the system, beyond the "world" as it is. While the fools form an army of *rebels, revolutionaries, to keep their ideal alive in the wake of all opposing ideas being eliminated, the faint candle people speak words of stopping wars, of embracing diversity, of ending the influence of the fools in charge. The way this light works is that one by one people become enlightened and can no longer be led around by the fools. Once you see it, you can't un-see it.*

Inner well

Tao Te Ching 06 - - - - - - - - *To **discover your spiritual spring** is to learn the secret of heaven and earth. In this mysterious spring, spirit is eternally present in eternal becoming.*

Vatthupama Sutta 20 - - - - - - - - *It is in this **inner spring** that you should bathe to convert yourself into a refuge for all beings. If you speak no lies and never harm living beings and never take what has not been given to you and abide in a faith that is free from greed, then what need do you have of finding a holy stream—any well will be your holy water source.*

Maha-Assapura Sutta 16 - - - - - - - - *Develop **self-confidence and singleness of mind** without applied and sustained thought, with rapture and pleasures born of concentration—as though there exists **a lake whose waters well up from below** without any streams entering it and without any rain ever falling upon it.*

Sotapattisamyutta 38 - - - - - - - - *As rain pours down in drops on a mountain top, flowing downward to fill the cracks, gullies, and creeks, filling pools, filling lakes, filling streams, flowing into rivers, filling up the great ocean—so too a noble disciple, with **confirmed confidence** in the Buddha, the **Dharma**, and the Sangha, along with the virtues dear to the noble ones, **flows onwards and beyond** to the destruction of the taints.*

John 4:13-14   Jesus answered and said unto her, Whosoever drinketh of this water shall thirst again: But whosoever drinketh of the water that I shall give him shall never thirst, but the water that I shall give him shall be in him a well of water springing up into everlasting life.

You can pass it along. You can now inspire others. Trickle down enlightenment.

Right views: right actions

Potaliya Sutta 4 - - - - - - - - *The Noble Discipline that leads to the cutting off of affairs—**refrain from the killing** of living beings, refrain from taking what has not been rightfully given to you, refrain from speaking falsely, refrain from speaking maliciously, refrain from rapacious greed, refrain from spiteful scolding, refrain from angry despair, and refrain from arrogance.*

Khuddakapatha 2 - - - - - - - - **Refrain from killing**, *from taking what is not given to you, from being unchaste, from speaking falsehoods, and from being swayed by gold and silver.*

Matthew 5:21 Ye have heard that it was said of them of old time, Thou shalt not kill; and whosoever shall kill shall be in danger of the judgment:

"Right actions" is one of the Noble Eightfold Path spokes to the **Dharma** *Wheel of Enlightenment. Right view is another. The whole shining of the Light is followed by exposing the Actions that are offensive.*

In the 1960s, the revival of Buddhist thought in the Western world that began in a trickle of poetry from the Beatniks, got sloganized in the Hippie (hip meaning enlightened, hip to how things really are) movement as "peace and love" and while "sex and drugs and rock n roll" had its considerations, the end result of this wave of individuals thinking outside the box of the system at hand was the anti-war protests. Give peace a chance. War is over if you want it.

No one thinks it is right to kill one of their own, but once they label other people as the enemy, as the problem, as the opposition to their religion and their heritage and their dreams, then they can justify killing in the context of war. The Godless Commies have to die before they come to America and make us all Red. Before that, religion was an important factor in witch hunts, in taking over heathen lands with the Manifest Destiny idea, Conquistadors, Crusades, Inquisitions.

Meanwhile, back in the second century, in the swelling wave of Simon bar Kokhba rallying for war support, the few defiant lights, the conscientious objectors, the damn Hippies, reveal the obvious: war is not good. Stop the killing.

Right intentions

Mahagopalaka Sutta 06-07 - - - - - - - - *When unwholesome states have arisen, and they are tolerated and not abandoned, not removed, not done away with, not annihilated, they* **accumulate like flies' eggs**. *Not being picked out, not being taken care of, forms seen and grasped at, their signs and features contemplated,* **the eye is left unguarded**. *This leaves opportunity for growth of unwholesome states of covetousness leading to grief.*

Mahagopalaka Sutta 19 - - - - - - - - **Pick out the flies' eggs**. *When a thought of sensual desire has arisen, do not tolerate it, abandon it, remove it, do away with it, and annihilate it.*

Vitakkasanthana Sutta 5 - - - - - - - - *A man with good eyes who doesn't want to see what is in front of his face can either shut his eyes or look away.*

Matthew 5:28-29 But I say unto you, That whosoever looketh on a woman to lust after her hath committed adultery with her already in his heart. And if thy right eye offend thee, pluck it out, and cast it from thee: for it is profitable for thee that one of thy members should perish, and not that thy whole body should be cast into hell.

Media fills the eyes with propaganda. If they can control what you want, they own you. You want this sexy woman. You want to drive this sexy car. You want to live in this sexy house. As long as there is something out there they can tease you with enough to make you change your focus, you are getting that glazed over Zombie look again. What if we did join up and fight and win this war and own the place like kings, surrounded by wine, women, and song? Wouldn't the goal be worth the risk? Best to just pluck the idea out of your head and move along before you get into trouble. Taking vows of celibacy is one thing in common between Buddhist monks and Christian monks and early Gnostics.

I think the topic is much deeper than whether to live alone or not. In much of the world to this day there is a "rape culture" mindset that views women as objects of conquest, as possessions, as a different form of conquering and dominance. The powerful against the powerless. When this mindset is propagated, endorsed, condoned, that is what builds up like dirt in the eyes preventing us from seeing clearly. Seeing injustice and violence and oppression and the effect these things have on women living in a "rape culture" situation, how can one who is Enlightened participate in the objectification of women? It is yet another game that we have to stop playing, and stop pretending that it is not a problem.

Right speech

Saccasamyutta 10 - - - - - - - - *Do not engage in* **the many forms of pointless talking**—*of kings, criminals, politicians, armies, dangers, wars, food, drink, clothes, beds, flowers, perfumes, relatives, vehicles, villages, towns, cities, countries, women, heroes. They talk on the street and by the well. They talk about days gone by, rambling chitchat, and speculation, about everything on land and in the sea. They are always talking about this and that.*

Matthew 5:34-37 But I say unto you, Swear not at all; neither by heaven; for it is God's throne: Nor by the earth; for it is his footstool: neither by Jerusalem; for it is the city of the great King. Neither shalt thou swear by thy head, because thou canst not make one hair white or black. But let your communication be, Yea, yea; Nay, nay: for whatsoever is more than these cometh of evil.

The great King. The only great King ruling over Jerusalem at that time would be Caesar. Simon had sworn to rule from Jerusalem, but it did not belong to him. He could swear all he wanted to and that would not change things. He could summon the sky but Zeus would not come to his aid. He could summon his faithful to gather from around the world, but that would only amount to not enough to take a stand upon. Stop with all the big words like you are so important. You aren't a magician. You aren't the Chosen One.

Quietness, monastic vows of silence, the lack of participating in what is commonly talked about is a spiritual trait in various cultures and ages. It is a world of media topics taking over the mindset of so many. Talks of blaming some president, of political views that can enrapture the mind to where there is nothing but such talk. Talks of sports, of the latest trends, of celebrities, of what was on the news. Words are powerful tools and traps, prayers and superstitions, subconscious signals distinguishing locals from foreigners. People spend a great deal of effort repeating back words about things that they know very little about. To swear that you have the answers, the complete truth of the matter, the inside scoop, is just a mind game that snares you in its trap. You don't know. You haven't considered everything. You haven't thought outside of the box that they taught you to think in. You find you choose your words from within the programming they imposed upon you, your so-called education. You really don't know. You are really a-gnostic if you are honest about it. You don't really understand so very much at all. Not the spiritual stuff like God sitting on a throne in heaven. So many words, but nobody knows. It may be true or not. It is just speculation. Expert on the world, the planet you are standing on? Have you been to the depths of the oceans? Have you climbed to the heights of the mountains? Have you looked at life through a microscope? Have you looked at life frozen in stone from millions of years back? Have you been places where everything is so vastly different, the people, the language, the customs, that you know nothing about them? Expert on the city you thought you knew? It belongs to Caesar now, the great King, it is completely different, things evolve and change and can you keep up with all of that? You are not even an expert when it comes to your own body, your own head, not even one single hair. There is so much you don't know. Those who speak do not know. Those who know speak very little. Enlightened are the quiet ones who disengage from conversations with the jibber jabbering idiots.

Right interaction: Practical Dharma

Mind control is the ability to deal with ill will. Mind release is the ability to encapsulate love. When you are open to change, the possibilities to just how far you can change is amazing. You can take actions you normally wouldn't take, speak thoughts that you normally wouldn't verbalize, start working on projects that you normally wouldn't have joined. Practical **Dharma***.*

This is a really long list of quotes. What that means is that this is a concentrated effort to gather together a lot of really amazing insights by the Buddha that were relayed by Jesus into the Gospel teaching collection.

*Upakkilesa Sutta 6 - - - - - - - - He abused me, he struck me, he defeated me, he robbed me—***in those who give a home to such feelings hatred will never be conquered***. In this world hatred is never conquered by further acts of hate. It is conquered by hating hate itself. This is an ancient* **Dharma** *carved in stone.*

Dhammapada 15:01-03 - - - - - - - - We should live with joy and love among those who hate. We should live with joy and health among those who are ill. We should **live in joy and peace among those who dwell on conflict***.*

Bojjhangasamyutta 51 - - - - - - - - There is the **liberation of mind through love***. Frequently giving careful attention to it is the poison that prevents new ill will from growing and existing ill will from thriving.*

Udanavarga 33:46 - - - - - - - - **Be tolerant** *with the intolerant.* **Be patient** *with the harsh. The holy man shows compassion to all creatures.*

Dhammapada 17:03 - - - - - - - - To anger, **respond with peacefulness***. To evil, respond with good. To greed, respond with giving. To lies, respond with truth.*

Dhammapada 01:05 - - - - - - - - Responding with more hate never defeats hate. Even in this world, **hate can be conquered only by compassion***. This is the Eternal* **Dharma***.*

Kakacupama Sutta 06 - - - - - - - - You should train yourself to remain unaffected of mind, without uttering any evil words, abiding with compassion for the welfare of others, with a mind of loving kindness, **with no trace of inner hate***. If anyone should give you a* *blow with his hand, with a rock, with a stick, or with a knife, you should **abandon any revengeful thoughts or words**.*

*Kakacupama Sutta 11 - - - - - - - - With minds remaining unaffected, we should never speak harshly. We should be actively compassionate for the welfare of others. We should possess a mindset of loving-kindness, with no trace of hidden spite. We shall live facing one another with a mind immersed in loving-kindness, and **starting with the person next to us, we shall live facing the entire planet with a mind immersed in loving-kindness**. In abundance, exalted, without limit, without hostility, without ill will, we should thus train ourselves.*

*Cittasamyutta 7 - - - - - - - - Above, below, across—everywhere, to all as to yourself, **dwell pervading the entire planet with a mind balanced in love**, abundant, exalted, and limitless, with no traces of any hostility or ill will.*

*Metta Sutta 7 - - - - - - - - As a mother protects her child at the stake of her own life, you must develop a generous heart for all others. Allow your state of **generous love to spread about to the entire globe**.*

*Sotapattisamyutta 06 - - - - - - - - Possess a mind devoid of the stain of stinginess, being freely generous, open-handed, delighting in relinquishment, **devoted to charity, delighting in giving and sharing**.*

Matthew 5:39-44 But I say unto you, That ye resist not evil: but whosoever shall smite thee on thy right cheek, turn to him the other also. And if any man will sue thee at the law, and take away thy coat, let him have thy cloak also. And whosoever shall compel thee to go a mile, go with him twain. Give to him that asketh thee, and from him that would borrow of thee turn not thou away. Ye have heard that it hath been said, Thou shalt love thy neighbour, and hate thine enemy. But I say unto you, Love your enemies, [bless them that curse you, do good to them that hate you,] and pray for them which [despitefully use you, and] persecute you;

What if the inheriting the earth is accomplished by love? Not by who has the biggest army. Not by who builds the tallest walls to protect their precious city. What if eventually the world is one global community of diversities working together in compassion and harmony?

There was this sense of being trapped in an overshadowing from the Roman Empire in occupation, from the other religious and philosophical ideas from the Greek speaking world, from being lost in the mix of a changing world that cares nothing for a frustrated people looking out with fear and loathing for their problem. The problem was that the world out there did not share their values, their superstitions, their clinging to ancient ideas and traditions. Theirs was a history of conflict, of dividing the world between good and evil, light and dark, us and them, saved and damned. When seen through this lens, every encounter with a Roman brought up visions of abuse, expectations of violent outbursts. The history of repeated defeats and suppressions of any group who stood up against these foreign bullies stayed in mind. The thought that they were robbing, taxing, imposing, demanding, made them appear with faces of contempt. The reality of the situation was beside the point; the worst was thought in a prejudiced way.

Love the enemy? Sympathy for the devils? Allow their diversity to mix with the pure white milk and honey tradition? When their soldiers come to restore the peace, if you are not with the revolutionaries then how do you deal with the politics of war? They have a job to be done. Don't stand in their way. If they push you, don't push back. If they need a coat from you, give them the shirt off your back. If they demand your help, go that extra mile for them. If they need something from you, give it to them. Stop dividing the world between us and them, between neighbor and enemy. Learn compassion that shouts louder than the bigoted cursing, that transcends the fog of hate that they are all still breathing in. Care about the shepherds as much as you care about the sheep. Change your scope from one people, one tradition, to a cosmopolitan embrace of the world as a whole, of a future of hope for peaceful interactions between a diversity of peoples. This very string of thought is strong enough to bind and suppress the Messianic faith in Simon bar Kokhba. Pure Anti-Christ heresy at its finest.

Rain and sun

*Lotus Sutra 05 - - - - - - - - The massive **clouds pour rain on all**, both the great and the small. The **sunlight and moonlight shine upon the entire world**, upon the good and the evil, upon the valued and the worthless. [...] I appear in the world like a large cloud that rains upon all of the dry withered sentient beings. This is so they can escape suffering, attain the joy of peace and assurance with the joys of this world and the joys of nirvana. [...] At all times and for all beings I preach the **Dharma** the same way, as I would for any person. [...] I offer a satisfied completion to the world, as the rain spreads moisture all around, to the great and the low, to the good and the evil, to the wise and the foolish.*

Matthew 5:45 That ye may be the children of your Father which is in heaven: for he maketh his sun to rise on the evil and on the good, and sendeth rain on the just and on the unjust.

*This one is such a direct quote that it illustrates the link between Buddhist missionary work in the Western World and the origins of the Jesus tradition. Mahayana Buddhist was a new form of thought, the Lotus Sutra being a window into this philosophy that saw itself as the Greater Vehicle for spreading the **Dharma** of the Buddha to the various cultures of the world.*

In the onset of a very violent and costly war with a great deal of suffering, an alternative, an antidote was just the ticket. The Answer had to be something very simple and common, available to everyone, instantly obvious, refreshing, enlightening. The idea of Peace can take hold and nothing else matters. All of the reasons for the holy war don't stand up to the gut feeling that Peace would be better for all.

*The "Father which is in heaven" is contrasted to the God of Simon. Simon's God supported the Chosen People and hates the Romans. Who is the Father which Jesus speaks of? If we do link this back to Buddhist tradition, the "Father" is Buddha and his heaven is Pure Land. This takes the scope far beyond that of a tribal god and a tradition for one particular people. The same **Dharma** empowers us all, no matter who we are and where we come from.*

Rain and sun, water and light, are elemental requirements, common to us all. Instead of focusing upon the differences, if we find the commonalities then we discover we are mostly the same. We are all living very similar lives. All of the words and fears and distinctions we have collected make us seem different, but none of that stuff is what ultimately matters.

Perfection

*Sotapattisamyutta 01 - - - - - - - - An **important king** that ruled over four continents died. Not possessing four things he is not freed from a bad fate. A **starving beggar** wearing rags that possesses four things is freed from a bad fate. The four are—confidence in the Buddha, confidence in the **Dharma**, confidence in the Sangha, and the practice of virtues dear to the noble ones.*

Luke 16:19-23 There was a certain rich man, which was clothed in purple and fine linen, and fared sumptuously every day: And there was a certain beggar named Lazarus, which was laid at his gate, full of sores, And desiring to be fed with the crumbs which fell from the rich man's table: moreover the dogs came and licked his sores. And it came to pass, that the beggar died, and was carried by the angels into Abraham's bosom: the rich man also died, and was buried; And in hell he lift up his eyes, being in torments, and seeth Abraham afar off, and Lazarus in his bosom.

*The king is named "Neuys" in the p75 version, meaning foolish. The king with all his worldly wealth and power is contrasted to a poor man who has discovered what is really to be treasured. The king's collected wealth doesn't comfort him in death. The poor man's **Dharma** takes him to heart. To attain Brahma, the idea of the one ultimate destination God, was the goal of the Hindu faithful which had come to listen to Siddhartha the Buddha. Union with God is such a powerful thought that Buddha used it as a vehicle for expressing his **Dharma**. You can't collect enough wealth to buy such a connection, but you can follow the path that will ultimately lead you there. Abraham's bosom is Brahma's heart. The similarity of the words Abraham and Brahma should be obvious.*

*Tevijja Sutta 39 - - - - - - - - The ascetic Gautama teaches **The Way to union with Brahma**.*

John 17:21 That they all may be one; as thou, Father, art in me, and I in thee, that they also may be one in us: that the world may believe that thou hast sent me.

Lotus Sutra 15 - - - - - - - - Ever since the long distant past, I have been teaching and converting the many.

John 8:56-58 Your father Abraham rejoiced to see my day: and he saw it, and was glad. Then said the Jews unto him, Thou art not yet fifty years old, and hast thou seen Abraham? Jesus said unto them, Verily, verily, I say unto you, Before Abraham was, I am.

There is this eternal power play struggle of ideologies, of world views. Is Buddha older than Brahma? Is Jesus older than Abraham?

*Culasaccaka Sutta 26 - - - - - - - - The liberated mind possesses three unsurpassable qualities—**perfect vision**, perfect practice of the way, and perfect deliverance.*

*Salayatanasamyutta 132 - - - - - - - - A mind well concentrated, clear and blemish free, loving towards all sentient beings—this is the way for **attaining Brahma**.*

Matthew 5:48 Be ye therefore perfect, even as your Father which is in heaven is perfect.

Perfection comes from beyond all this, perhaps in some imagined Platonic ideal, but for it to mean anything it gets integrated into real life, into vision, into practice, into deliverance.

*Samanamandika Sutta 11 - - - - - - - - You who are truly virtuous **do not identify with your virtue**.*

Matthew 6:2-4 Therefore when thou doest thine alms, do not sound a trumpet before thee, as the hypocrites do in the synagogues and in the streets, that they may have glory of men. Verily I say unto you, They have their reward. But when thou doest alms, let not thy left hand know what thy right hand doeth: That thine alms may be in secret: and thy Father which seeth in secret himself shall reward thee openly.

Tao Te Ching 47 - - - - - - - - Go into your room. Keep the door closed. Know the secrets of the world. Shut the window. Observe The Way of Heaven. The further you explore, the less you know.

Matthew 6:6 But thou, when thou prayest, enter into thy closet, and when thou hast shut thy door, pray to thy Father which is in secret; and thy Father which seeth in secret shall reward thee [openly].

*Sakkasamyutta 24 - - - - - - - - There are two types of fools. One does not see a wrong as a wrong. The other does not **forgive one who is sorry** for a wrong.*

Matthew 6:14-15 For if ye forgive men their trespasses, your heavenly Father will also forgive you: But if ye forgive not men their trespasses, neither will your Father forgive your trespasses.

Perfection. You have reached perfection, touched perfection, mystically merged into oneness with perfection. But don't let this *"perfect in God" idea go to your head. No need to be all "look at me, I got it" proud. No need to be so out in the open about your mysticism. Not need to be so judgmental and unforgiving at those who haven't yet woken up to your newly discovered truth.*

Keep your Gnostic status safely hidden away in the closet. If you are being all cosmopolitan around people who are still stuck in the limited scope of antiquated ideas, they cannot understand you, they cannot paradigm shift enough to consider your position. Who is this "Father which is in secret" as contrasted with the structures of organized religion and public gatherings?

No Chosen People, no superior race. Also, no special individual perfect people, no infallible popes, no unquestioned politicians. Don't believe the hype and don't follow leaders. Lower the hills and raise the valleys to make a level playing field for all, on a national level and on an individual level. Education for all. End special privilege for any. Desegregate the world into one cosmopolitan union. Knock down those who stand themselves up as superior. Help back to their feet those who have fallen behind. Removing the delusions of divisions is difficult because they are so embedded in the way we think, our prejudices, our assumptions, our blind faith in traditional ideas. If everyone sees everyone else on a level playing field of mutual respect, that changes everything. No more masters and slaves, owners and workers, rulers and ruled, rich and poor, privileged class and untouchables, saved and damned, light and dark, us and them. All these distinctions shrink into the background blur of details while the focus shifts to the cosmopolitan oneness of humanity. This dream is very dangerous to those who are trying to keep all the old reasons for war alive in the minds of those they have brainwashed into thinking they are the Chosen People and Simon is the Messiah.

This concept of no one is better is a powerful thought. What makes people think they are better? Racial heritage; wealth of family; respect and assigned position; physical strength; physical beauty; spiritual insights? They all wash away in the rain. All are outshined by the sun.

Idea bombs, spreading by contact, transmitted in little word packets, little memes of wisdom, rippling across the people, each taking on a life of their own. Judge a stock by its performance. Sell the shares in what you see is going to crash. Buy more shares of what you see is going to prosper. Use the same "judgement call" technique in collecting or eliminating ideas.

Values adjustment

Anangana Sutta 15 - - - - - - - - *It is possible that a disciple may wish to **get the best** seat, the best water, and the best food in the house, instead of another disciple. It is possible that some other disciple ends up with the best seat, or the best water, or the best food in the house. The anger and the bitterness become like open sores. It is possible that a disciple may wish to get the most beautiful robe, instead of another disciple. It is possible that some other disciple ends up with the most beautiful robe. The **anger and the bitterness** become like open sores.*

Devatasamyutta 51 - - - - - - - - *Wisdom is the precious gem of humanity. **Thieves** cannot steal merit.*

Tao Te Ching 53 - - - - - - - - *To dress richly, to collect weapons, and to indulge in sensual excess and wealth, are just invitations to the **robbers**.*

Mahadukkhakklandha Sutta 10 - - - - - - - - *If a workingman comes into possessing wealth, he will experience pain and grief in protecting it. How can he keep it from being taxed by the government, or stolen by **thieves**, or burned by fire, or washed away by flood, or stolen by relatives? He guards and protects, sorrows, grieves, laments, until finally he beats himself in distress saying he wishes he never had it.*

Khuddakapatha 8:9 - - - - - - - - *The wise man will act righteously, creating for himself a treasure that no one can **steal**, and that cannot **rust** away.*

Udanavarga 01:21-22 - - - - - - - - *Though you possess hundreds of thousands of worldly possessions, you are still subject to death. **All collections will be dispersed**. All pile-ups will be thrown down. All assemblies will be taken apart. All life must end in death.*

Vangisasamyutta 2 - - - - - - - - *Vangisa—Whatever exists here on earth occupying space, composed of form, part of the world—**it is all impermanent, it all decays**. You live as a sage once you have penetrated this truth. People are bound to their possessions—to what they can see and hear, sense and feel. Abandoning desire, unmoved, you are a sage who clings to nothing around yourself.*

Tao Te Ching 03 - - - - - - - - *If the Perfect Sage wishes to convince people to abandon concerns over wealth,* **he should not himself value expensive items**.

Tevijjavacchagotta Sutta 11 - - - - - - - - *No one who* **owns a house**, *who doesn't abandon the fetter of concern for the house, on the death of the body has come to the state of having* **extinguished suffering**.

Dvedhavitakka Sutta 06 - - - - - - - - *Whatever you frequently think of and ponder upon, that* **defines the inclination of your mind**.

Khandhasamyutta 36 - - - - - - - - *If you have an underlying tendency toward something, then you are measured in accordance with it. If you are measured in accordance with something, then* **you are defined in terms of it**.

Dhammapada 21:01 - - - - - - - - *If it is possible to forsake a limited pleasure and thus discover eternal happiness,* **the wise will abandon the limited pleasure** *seeking the eternal happiness*.

Devatasamyutta 41 - - - - - - - - *When your house is on fire, you salvage what you need, leaving the rest to become burnt. The world is on fire with aging and death. You must rescue by giving.* **What is given is what is salvaged**. *What is given produces good fruit. What is kept is not fruitful. It is taken by thieves and governments, lost in the fire and burnt.*

Dhammapada 13:11 - - - - - - - - *The greedy do not make it to heaven, those fools who shun charity.* **The wise who give freely will find much happiness for eternity**.

Lotus Sutra 18 - - - - - - - - **Nothing in this world is lasting. Don't think of possessions as being stones. Think of them like foamy bubbles, shimmering and then evaporating. You must learn to quickly let go of it all and go along your way**.

Ratthapala Sutta 42 - - - - - - - - *I see wealthy men of this world in ignorance failing to share from their gathered wealth. Greedily they hoard their riches away, still trapped by longings for more sensual pleasures. [...]* **As he dies nothing can follow him, not child, not wife, not wealth, not royal estate**.

Ratthapala Sutta 22 - - - - - - - - *Follow my advice and have your pile of gold loaded on carts and dumped into a river. For on account of gold there arises for you sorrow, lamentation, pain, grief, and despair.*

Matthew 6:19-21   Lay not up for yourselves treasures upon earth, where moth and rust doth corrupt, and where thieves break through and steal: But lay up for yourselves treasures in heaven, where neither moth nor rust doth corrupt, and where thieves do not break through nor steal: For where your treasure is, there will your heart be also.

Luke 12:16-21   And he spake a parable unto them, saying, The ground of a certain rich man brought forth plentifully: And he thought within himself, saying, What shall I do, because I have no room where to bestow my fruits? And he said, This will I do: I will pull down my barns, and build greater; and there will I bestow all my fruits and my goods. And I will say to my soul, Soul, thou hast much goods laid up for many years; take thine ease, eat, drink, and be merry. But God said unto him, Thou fool, this night thy soul shall be required of thee: then whose shall those things be, which thou hast provided? So is he that layeth up treasure for himself, and is not rich toward God.

You can't take it with you. You can collect houses and cars and boats and toys and investment accounts and businesses, and your kids can deal with the assets and debts after you are dead, but none of that is really yours.

Let it go. Give up the prize and then there's no need for the battle. Once you release your grip, the tug of war is over for you. Once you are no longer one of them, it no longer matters what they think of you.

The rust and thieves references along with the Stoic tone of these verses link back to the Buddhist thoughts. Part of the revolution is to establish pecking order in life, rewrite the organization chart of who is in charge of what, who owns what, and whoever dies with the biggest pile of stuff is the winner. What Jesus, and Buddha and Lao Tzu, here are suggesting is that the biggest pile does not make you the winner, it rather makes you to have lived a life under the thumb of the Almighty Dollar.

What do people struggle for? A fancier place to sit with a different kind of lunch? Driven by ambition, angry and bitter at the competition, what it takes to collect enough Money becomes a self-imposed trap. Got that paycheck. Then comes the government wanting taxes taken out. What you buy with it can get stolen by thieves, and if you manage to escape ever having a major fire or flood, what hasn't rusted away or become obsoleted into worthlessness is dispersed to the relatives after you're dead. It is all uncollected, the piles knocked down, the assembled collections of stuff taken apart and auctioned off or discarded.

Homelessness is the opposite of conquest. They, Simon's supporters, hold up Chosen People owning the Promised Land, ruling from the Sacred City, God living in their Golden Temple. They fight a revolution for this dream with violent acts of terrorism, xenophobic fury and frenzy, Messianic hopes held onto with a blind faith that they will be the winners and the end result is that they gain all of the possessions now claimed by the foreigners. The Jesus alternative, the antidote, is to want no land, no home, no possessions, no conquests, no sacred temple, and no god that lives in a house. The poverty response disarms the reason for the war. When there is a war, lots of reasons can be presented but it almost always comes down to money, who can profit the most from fighting and winning the war? What if profit and winning are taken out of the equation?

Widow's mites

Devatasamyutta 32 - - - - - - - - *Some provide from the little they have. Others are rich and hold back on their giving.* **An offering given from what little you have is worth a thousand times its actual value.**

Luke 21:1-4   And he looked up, and saw the rich men casting their gifts into the treasury. And he saw also a certain poor widow casting in thither two mites. And he said, Of a truth I say unto you, that this poor widow hath cast in more than they all: For all these have of their abundance cast in unto the offerings of God: but she of her penury hath cast in all the living that she had.

Those focused

Ariyapariyesana Sutta 20 - - - - - - - - *There are* **those with little dust in their eyes** *who are missing out on being able to hear the* **Dharma**. *[...] Let the Blessed One teach the* **Dharma**. *There will be those who can understand.*

Salayatanasamyutta 228 - - - - - - - - **The eye is the ocean for a person**. *Forms are its currents. You who stand firm in the midst of the currents of forms are said to have transcended the ocean of the eye with its waves, whirlpools, sharks, and sea serpents. Crossed over, gone beyond, the Brahmin stands on high ground.*

Matthew 6:22-23 The light of the body is the eye: if therefore thine eye be single, thy whole body shall be full of light. But if thine eye be evil, thy whole body shall be full of darkness. If therefore the light that is in thee be darkness, how great is that darkness!

The whole world is not beyond hope. Some can "see" what you're talking about. Some can focus on your vision and get it. Most can't see straight, can't see what's obviously right in front of them. The world comes through in waves and whirlpools, pushing them this way and that, tossing them around in circles. And then there are the monsters, like the dogs of war, that manipulate through visions of fear and hate and duty and faith. It is easy for the Enlightened to see past all of that, but not for those trapped in their darkened world.

Life gratification

Alagaddupama Sutta 03 - - - - - - - - *Sensual pleasures provide you with* **little real gratification**. *Instead, they bring* **much suffering, despair, and danger**.

Sotapattisamyutta 54 - - - - - - - - *Are you anxious about your mother and father? Are you anxious about your wife and children?* **Whether or not you are anxious, you will die anyway**. *So please abandon your anxiety. [...] Are you anxious about what pleasures you can sense as a human?* **Celestial pleasures sensed are more excellent and sublime**.

Matthew 6:25 Therefore I say unto you, Take no thought for your life, what ye shall eat, or what ye shall drink; nor yet for your body, what ye shall put on. Is not the life more than meat, and the body than raiment?

Life conclusion

*Ratthapala Sutta 42 - - - - - - - - A **longer lifespan** is not purchased by wealth. Prosperity cannot banish **getting old**. This life is short, the sages understand. It cannot know eternity, **only change**. The rich and poor alike touch their end. The fool and sage as well feel it. While the fool is stricken by folly, no sage will ever tremble at the touch of their end. Better is wisdom for this reason than amassing wealth, since **wisdom is the price of the final goal**.*

Matthew 6:27-30 Which of you by taking thought can add one cubit unto his stature? And why take ye thought for raiment? Consider the lilies of the field, how they grow; they toil not, neither do they spin: And yet I say unto you, That even Solomon in all his glory was not arrayed like one of these. Wherefore, if God so clothe the grass of the field, which to day is, and to morrow is cast into the oven, shall he not much more clothe you, O ye of little faith?

The flying hour

Bhaddekaratta Sutta 3 - - - - - - - - **Don't dwell on the past or live in hopes for the future**. *The past it is gone. The future has not yet arrived. Instead, look with insight into each presently arisen state. Know it. Be sure of it.* **Without thought of failure, or being shaken off course**, *put your effort into today. You may be dead tomorrow. No bargaining with death can hold its overwhelming arrival. But you who can* **live passionately and relentlessly with each present day**, *each present night, your death will remain a single excellent night.*

Matthew 6:34   Take therefore no thought for the morrow: for the morrow shall take thought for the things of itself. Sufficient unto the day is the evil thereof.

If you live in the past or get trapped in a puddle of "what ifs" for the future, tradition and prophecy, heritage and politics for the future, this chain will keep you from being alive this very day. Break the chain of time. Jump off their bandwagon and take the alternative fresh start. No past foundation. No known future to envision. Just living with enough passion and guts and determination and direction to live out each day in an excellence that they can never understand.

Karma

Culakammavibhanga Sutta 14 - - - - - - - - *You who give food, drink, clothing, transportation, pleasant surroundings, beds, homes, or lights to the homeless, wherever reborn will be wealthy.*

Matthew 7:2 For with what judgment ye judge, ye shall be judged: and with what measure ye mete, it shall be measured to you again.

What goes around, comes around. You reap what you sow. And in the end the love you take is equal to the love you make.

Observant to a fault

Vitakkasanthana Sutta 3 - - - - - - - - *A skilled carpenter might knock out and extract a **coarse peg** by means of a smaller peg.*

Salayatanasamyutta 090 - - - - - - - - *Being stirred is a disease, a tumor, and a dart. This is why the Tathagata lives unstirred, with **the dart extracted**.*

Udanavarga 27:01; Dhammapada 18:18 - - - - - - - - *It is easier to see the faults of others than one's own. One tends to flaunt the faults of others while **concealing one's own faults**.*

Dhammapada 04:07 - - - - - - - - *Do not dwell on the faults of others, what they have done or have failed to do. **Dwell on what you yourself have done and have failed to do**.*

Matthew 7:3-5 And why beholdest thou the mote that is in thy brother's eye, but considerest not the beam that is in thine own eye? Or how wilt thou say to thy brother, Let me pull out the mote out of thine eye; and, behold, a beam is in thine own eye? Thou hypocrite, first cast out the beam out of thine own eye; and then shalt thou see clearly to cast out the mote out of thy brother's eye.

Focus on your own spiritual journey. Lose your own bad habits. Conquer your own inner demons. Guard your own Zen state of mind. Not everyone is ready to advance. Not everyone wants their faults highlighted. Not everyone wants to hear about your meditation techniques, your aha moments, or any of the details of your own personal spiritual journey. It is like living in a bubble in a way, a bubble that floats through the world but doesn't pause to judgingly challenge or recklessly offer to help others change into living in bubbles themselves. Those destined for the bubble life will find it and you may can help them, but you will be in a better state to help them if you get your own mind focused and cleansed of antiquated ideas and blind faith justifications for perpetuating a lack of sympathy and charity.

Lotus Sutra 14 - - - - - - - - *Considered as a bright jewel given from a king, this sutra is to be highly honored. As such it is to be constantly **guarded and protected and not recklessly revealed**.*

Matthew 7:6 Give not that which is holy unto the dogs, neither cast ye your pearls before swine, lest they trample them under their feet, and turn again and rend you.

You don't take sacred items and let the dogs play with them. You don't hang a string of pearls on a pig. You don't go around shouting about peace and saying folks should avoid the war around Simon's people. They will kick your ideas to the ground and turn around and kill you. Such a precarious position to be a peaceful monk in a world recruiting soldiers.

Guaranteed to eventually arrive at the truth

Canki Sutta 22 - - - - - - - - *Striving is the best thing you can do to finally arrive at the truth.* **If you do not strive, you will never arrive** *at the truth. Because you strive, you are guaranteed to eventually arrive at the truth. This is why striving is the best thing you can do to finally arrive at the truth.*

Matthew 7:7-8 Ask, and it shall be given you; seek, and ye shall find; knock, and it shall be opened unto you: For every one that asketh receiveth; and he that seeketh findeth; and to him that knocketh it shall be opened.

Golden rule

Kosalasamyutta 08 - - - - - - - - Each person treats himself very dearly. Just as you would not harm yourself, **you should not harm others**.

Matthew 7:11-12 : If ye then, being evil, know how to give good gifts unto your children, how much more shall your Father which is in heaven give good things to them that ask him? Therefore all things whatsoever ye would that men should do to you, do ye even so to them: for this is the law and the prophets.

The golden rule applies to everyone, "us" and "them", family and stranger, "like" and "different". You want to understand what the law demands and what the prophets predict? What about: love is the law and the prophecy for the future is a world filled with love. Make that your religion and get enthused about it, why don't you?

Mind has two doorways; the crooked path and the smooth

Satipatthana Sutta 2 - - - - - - - - *Follow the* **Direct Path**.

Sallekha Sutta 14 - - - - - - - - *What if you saw an* **uneven path** *and another even path by which to avoid it? What if you came by boat to a* **rough stream** *and another smooth waterway by which to avoid it?*

Devaputtasamyutta 06 - - - - - - - - *Ignoble ones fall down head first into the* **crooked path**. *The path of the noble ones is smooth, even as the noble ones are smooth in the midst of the crooked.*

Awakening of Faith 3: 1 - - - - - - - - **The mind has two doorways** *through which it may venture. One leads to a realization of the mind's Pure Being. The other leads to the discriminations of what appears and disappears, of life and death.*

Devatasamyutta 46 - - - - - - - - *Resounding with a host of nymphs, haunted by a host of demons, this tangled forest of delusion—how do you escape from it? The* **straight way** *is the name of the path to the fearless destination. You may follow this way with the strong chariot riding on wheels made up of wholesome states. Disgust with what is wrong is its floorboard. Mindfulness is its seat.* **Dharma** *is the chariot driver. Right view is the horse. You who have found such a vehicle have the means to approach Nirvana.*

Satipatthanasamyutta 12 - - - - - - - - *The gatekeeper posted is wise, competent, and intelligent. He keeps out strangers and admits acquaintances. While he patrols the walls, he doesn't allow holes large enough for cats to slip through. He is assured that all large creatures that enter or leave this city do so from* **the one gate**.

Matthew 7:13-14 Enter ye in at the strait gate: for wide is the gate, and broad is the way, that leadeth to destruction, and many there be which go in thereat: Because strait is the gate, and narrow is the way, which leadeth unto life, and few there be that find it.

A small opening is a lens, zoomed in and focused.

Sheep's clothing

*Dhammapada 26:12 - - - - - - - - What good is **sheep's clothing**? Inwardly mangled they manage to make their appearance shine.*

Matthew 7:15 Beware of false prophets, which come to you in sheep's clothing, but inwardly they are ravening wolves.

Ever met people who are two-faced? They are so squeaky nice and polite but they are plotting against you behind your back? Project that onto organized religion. They want to appear like they want to save your soul, but what they really want to do is judge your ass. They are not the gatekeepers of anything you should wish to venture through.

Corrupt seed

Surangama Sutra - - - - - - - - *A **corrupt seed** will reveal itself in diseased and malformed fruit.*

Udanavarga 09:08 - - - - - - - - *Whatever a person does, be it good or evil, is never without consequence, for **all deeds bear fruit** of its own kind.*

Matthew 7:16-18 Ye shall know them by their fruits. Do men gather grapes of thorns, or figs of thistles? Even so every good tree bringeth forth good fruit; but a corrupt tree bringeth forth evil fruit. A good tree cannot bring forth evil fruit, neither can a corrupt tree bring forth good fruit.

Matthew 12:33-36 Either make the tree good, and his fruit good; or else make the tree corrupt, and his fruit corrupt: for the tree is known by his fruit. O generation of vipers, how can ye, being evil, speak good things? For out of the abundance of the heart the mouth speaketh. A good man out of the good treasure of the heart bringeth forth good things: and an evil man out of the evil treasure bringeth forth evil things. But I say unto you, That every idle word that men shall speak, they shall give account thereof in the day of judgment.

How to tell if someone is a good spiritual advisor or a bad one? It is the same way you tell if a fruit tree is good, take a sample of the fruit and you will know from the taste. If you can't stomach the advice, it is so obviously wrong, you have a gut feeling about it that repulses you, leaves you with thoughts of fear and loathing, then it is probably nothing you should be signing up for. Messiahs rallying for war. Gatherings for witch hunts, lynchings, inquisitions, crusades. If the fruit tastes rotten, there is something wrong with the religion.

I can only show them the Way

Ganakamoggallana Sutta 14 - - - - - - - - *Nirvana exists and the Way leading to Nirvana exists. I have come to show the Way. When I advise and instruct my disciples, some of them attain Nirvana, the ultimate goal, and others do not attain it. What can I do about that? I can only show them the Way.*

Satipatthanasamyutta 03 - - - - - - - - *Fools come up to make requests of me. I speak to them the* **Dharma**, *but they only think of following me around.*

Matthew 7:21 Not every one that saith unto me, Lord, Lord, shall enter into the kingdom of heaven; but he that doeth the will of my Father which is in heaven.

Luke 6:46 And why call ye me, Lord, Lord, and do not the things which I say?

This is an interesting comment, implying that Christianity formed that defines Jesus as "Lord" and yet doesn't center upon his teachings. The "doeth the will of my Father" is here replaced with the doing of what Jesus said.

Gamanisamyutta 06 - - - - - - - - *Suppose a person would hurl a huge boulder into a deep pool of water. Then a crowd would assemble around it and have prayers and praises and rituals with salutations, chanting "Come up out of the water great boulder. Ascend to higher ground great boulder". What do you think, because of the prayers of this great crowd of people, with their praises and rituals with salutations, would that boulder ascend to higher ground?*

James 2:17 Faith without works is dead.

Teachers don't want admiring fans, they want students that take the knowledge and put it to use. A music teacher wants to hear the students play music. A mechanical teacher wants to observer the students make their own repairs. A spiritual teacher likewise wants to watch the students advance and excel. Christianity became such a cult of worshipping Jesus; it has lost out on the focus of following the instructions of Jesus.

Luke 6.40 The disciple is not above his master: but every one that is perfect shall be as his master.

Be solid: good roof

Dhammapada 01:13-14 - - - - - - - - *As rain pours into a house with a bad roof, so passion pours into an uncultivated spirit. As no rain can enter a house with a **good roof**, so passion can find no way into a **cultivated spirit**.*

Be strong: a stand

Maggasamyutta 027 - - - - - - - - *A pot without a stand is easily knocked over. A pot with a stand is difficult to knock over. The mind without a stand is easily knocked over. **The mind with a stand is difficult to knock over**.*

Be substantial: weight

Saccasamyutta 39 - - - - - - - - *A tiny piece of cotton on the ground will be blown whichever way the wind blows. **A piece of iron on the ground will not shake**, quake, or tremble in the wind. It has weight and is secure in its place.*

Matthew 7:24-28 Therefore whosoever heareth these sayings of mine, and doeth them, I will liken him unto a wise man, which built his house upon a rock: And the rain descended, and the floods came, and the winds blew, and beat upon that house; and it fell not: for it was founded upon a rock. And every one that heareth these sayings of mine, and doeth them not, shall be likened unto a foolish man, which built his house upon the sand: And the rain descended, and the floods came, and the winds blew, and beat upon that house; and it fell: and great was the fall of it. [And it came to pass,] when Jesus had ended these sayings, the people were astonished at his doctrine:

Not being happy to call any place home

Dhammapada 07:02 - - - - - - - - *Those who have higher thoughts are always reaching out, not being happy to call any place home.*

Vanasamyutta 4 - - - - - - - - *As the deer roam free without ties, the bhikkhus live **homeless**.*

Matthew 8:20 And Jesus saith unto him, The foxes have holes, and the birds of the air have nests; but the Son of man hath not where to lay his head.

Reformed bandit

*Angulimala Sutta 2, 5, 11 - - - - - - - - A murderous bloody violent merciless killer laid waste to villages, towns, and districts. He constantly murdered people and made a garland of their fingers. [...] The bandit walked as fast as he could but could not catch up with the Blessed One who was casually walking. He stopped and called out to the Blessed One—stop, recluse! Buddha answered—I have stopped. You stop too. [...] Suppose you were to see **that bandit had shaved, dressed in a yellow robe, and entered the homeless life**. He abstains from killing living beings, from taking, from lying, from eating at night, from sexual pursuits, virtuous and of good character. If you saw him like this, how would you treat him?*

This is omitted from Matthew, found in Mark 5:15-16 and Luke 8:35-36

Luke 8:35-36 Then they went out to see what was done; and came to Jesus, and found the man, out of whom the devils were departed, sitting at the feet of Jesus, clothed, and in his right mind: and they were afraid. They also which saw it told them by what means he that was possessed of the devils was healed.

In the writings of Josephus, the Jews who fought against the Romans in the first century were called bandits, basically the same as "terrorists" in modern terms. Simon and his followers were extremely violent and killed off an entire legion of Roman soldiers. What if the most violent of them all, the Messiah Simon himself, were to embrace a being a pacifist monk lifestyle? Legion of devils, legion of soldiers, the veil on this story is thin enough for anyone to see through at the meaning of it being against the violence of war.

I forgive

Devatasamyutta 35 - - - - - - - - The enlightened one is full of compassion for all beings. For him there are no transgressions. For him there is no going astray. He is not lost in the confusion, but is wise and ever mindful. For if one does not forgive those who confess transgression, harboring anger, intending judgment, strongly establishing an enmity—this is a very undelightful state to be in. Thus **I forgive your transgressions**.

Matthew 9:6 But that ye may know that the Son of man hath power on earth to forgive sins, (then saith he to the sick of the palsy,) Arise, take up thy bed, and go unto thine house.

They make damnation and the need for forgiveness such a focal topic. Who's to bless and who's to blame? Only God can judge? Only his self-appointed representatives? Say three Hail Marys and make a donation. What can the average person do, the child of humanity, to absolve sin? What power do we have, what authority, what right, to set anyone free from the tyranny of Fascist justice, of the unexpected Spanish Inquisition, of the imagined fate of everlasting hell? Something or someone would have to bleed for that to work! You can't just go around and tell people that they can walk away from the mental funk of Organized Religion and it will all be OK! End the guilt trips, the anger, the judgment, the being unplugged from the family and society. End the rules and noticing who fails to follow the rules. End the cloud of confusion hovering over humanity like an incurable sickness. Announce wisdom and mindfulness and forgiveness. Empower people to take a stand and walk away from the mind game guilt trips that have been keeping them sick and disabled. Brother, get up and walk!

Dirty soiled garment

Magandiya Sutta 20-24 - - - - - - - - *A blind man went to search for white beautiful spotless clean clothing. He was deceived into accepting a **dirty soiled garment** to wear. One day he regained his sight and with it the desire to continue to wear that dirty soiled garment was abandoned. He burned it, thinking about killing the man that tricked him and cheated him.*

Vatthupama Sutta 02-03 - - - - - - - - *What if you took **an old rag**, ripped and stained, and dipped it into a bright color dye—blue, yellow, red, or pink. It would look improper. The color would not be uniform. When the mind starts out defiled, no happy result may be expected. The imperfections that defile the mind—covetousness, being selfish and greedy, ill will, anger, revenge, contempt, having a domineering attitude, jealousy, avarice, deceit, fraud, showy pride, presumption, conceit, arrogance, vanity, and a lack of compassion or empathy.*

Matthew 9:16 No man putteth a piece of new cloth unto an old garment, for that which is put in to fill it up taketh from the garment, and the rent is made worse.

New ideas are wasted on grumpy old farts. You can't patch the old system. You can't clean it. You can't dye it. It has to be abandoned. It is a relic from a different age. It no longer has any value. It is making you look bad and stupid and needs to be replaced with something better. You have been tricked into accepting the old garment for so long that when you get a gift of new material instead of thinking to make a new garment, you only think of using it to patch the old piece of rags you've been wearing. This is one of the most important parables of Jesus.

The system of thought you have been operating out of is defective. You have blind faith in lies that you have been deceived into accepting. You have been tricked and cheated.

Thomas 37 His disciples said, "When will you appear to us, and when will we see you?" Jesus said, "When you strip without being ashamed, and you take your clothes and put them under your feet like little children and trample then, then [you] will see the son of the living one and you will not be afraid."

You have to unpack all the baggage, undress from all the Fundamentalist Organized Religion self-righteous robe nonsense. There is no God Almighty to pray to so you can become rich or get your revenge on those you don't like. There is no God Almighty to support your blind faith in your superstitions at the expense of those who don't think like you. That old garment is only going to make you a target, a uniform of death. Take it off and never look back.

*Agnostic is the first step towards **Gnosis**. Doubting faith, unlearning what you discover to be untrue, apostate uncloaked direct Zen snapping out of it awakening. I may not know exactly what I believe, but I know for a fact that I no longer believe in that.*

Like a raft

Alagaddupama Sutta 13 - - - - - - - - **Dharma** *is like a raft— useful for* **crossing over**, *then useless to hold onto.*

Sallekha Sutta 12 - - - - - - - - *Do not adhere to possessed views or hold them stubbornly.* **Let go of them easily.** *Practice effacement.*

Matthew 9:17 Neither do men put new wine into old bottles: else the bottles break, and the wine runneth out, and the bottles perish: but they put new wine into new bottles, and both are preserved.

The new cannot be contained by the old. You can't fill up the old with the new and make the old now OK. The new requires a fresh start. Part of spiritually advancing is the need for ending chapters of your path and starting over. Smash the old bottles, discard them, let them go, set them on a shelf in a museum with captions that read this is how I once thought, just don't continue with the same old mindset. Don't append the New Testament onto the end of the Old Testament. It was an apt warning.

It is like building a raft to cross a river and it was fine and useful for crossing that river, but now it has to be left behind. You don't continue to carry the river raft through the journey through the desert or up the mountain. Let it go. Lose the old bottles.

Free of all doubt and hesitation

Lotus Sutra 17 - - - - - - - - If a person is completely free of all doubt and hesitation and from the depths of heart has an **instance of faith***, he will indeed be blessed.*

Matthew 9:22 But Jesus turned him about, and when he saw her, he said, Daughter, be of good comfort; thy faith hath made thee whole. And the woman was made whole from that hour.

Mind over matter is a powerful thing indeed.

Perfect holy medicine

Vimalakirtinirdesha Sutra 8 - - - - - - - - *In time of sickness, the pure bodhisattvas prescribe the perfect holy medicine,* **causing all to become healthy and joyful**, *freed from their sickness. In time of hunger, they offer food and drink, stopping hunger and thirst, thus teaching the* **Dharma** *to healthy beings.*

Matthew 9:35 And Jesus went about all the cities and villages, teaching in their synagogues, and preaching the gospel of the kingdom, and healing every sickness and every disease among the people.

Simon went about all the cities and villages preaching that he was the Star Child, leaving behind him a legacy of violence and starvation and useless blind faith. Random acts of violence. Organized hate for the Romans. Raising up a group mindset that supports this xenophobic quest for ethnic cleansing at the fevered pitch of faith over reason. Such waves of holy war faith continue to this day in various parts of the world in defense of and in opposition to various faiths.

What if the faith was in human potential for kindness, for compassion, for charity, for education? What if the faithful missionaries were not out there recruiting for a war effort, but were instead sharing a sense of human compassion that transcended divisions between us? Random acts of love. Organized compassion for all. Jesus here is the anti-Simon. The kingdom, the **Dharma**, *is the antidote for the Messianic faith that believes that Simon would defeat Caesar.*

Wander abroad for the good of the many

Mahapadana Sutta 3:26 - - - - - - - - *I send you forth, monks, to wander abroad for the good of the many, for the welfare and happiness of divas (angels, gods) and humans. Display the holy live fully complete and perfect. There are beings with little dust on their eyes that are perishing through not hearing* **Dharma**. *They will become knowers of* **Dharma**.

Mahavagga 1:11:1 - - - - - - - - *Walk, monks, across the lands so that the people may find blessing, so that the people may find joy, and **so that the people may find compassion**. Let not two of you follow the same path.*

Matthew 10:7-8 And as ye go, preach, saying, The kingdom of heaven is at hand. Heal the sick, cleanse the lepers, raise the dead, cast out devils: freely ye have received, freely give.

Blessing, joy, compassion. Compassion is the antidote for violent conflict. All is good. All is happy. All is love. All is healed. All is cleansed. All is alive. All is free from the mind games. War is over if you want it. Simon's kingdom will never be seen, but the kingdom of heaven is already here. If your victory is all in the mind, they have no amount of soldiers that can conquer it from you. Simon wanted to control Israel and banish all the Romans. Hadrian ended up controlling all "Palestine" and banishing all the Jews. The control of Jesus was a kingdom not of this world. Everyone's a winner. The meek have inherited the whole world through compassion. The kingdom of heaven is at hand.

Without possession

*Kandaraka Sutta 15; Culahatthipadopama Sutta 14; Surangama Sutra - - - - - - - - Content with the robe on your body, trusting in alms food to maintain your stomach, wherever you go, **taking nothing else with you**—Just as a bird, wherever it ventures, flies with only its wings to have to be carried.*

Matthew 10:9-10 Provide neither gold, nor silver, nor brass in your purses, Nor scrip for your journey, neither two coats, neither shoes, nor yet staves: for the workman is worthy of his meat.

The Essenes

Free as a bird. The networked support system of the Essenes as described by Philo and Josephus comes to mind here. This highlights that not all Jews thought like Simon and that there was an entire faction that was ready to accept teachings like that of Jesus. Without such a group, promoting a Jesus that was the antithesis of Simon would have fallen upon deaf ears. The Arabic word for Jesus is Isa, which is perhaps related to the word Essene (Isa-ene).

*Josephus: The Jewish War, Book 2, Chapter 8, Paragraph 4 (78 AD): They have no one certain city, but many of them dwell in every city; and if any of their sect come from other places, what they have lies open for them, just as if it were their own; and they go in to such as they never knew before, as if they had been ever so long acquainted with them. For which reason they carry nothing at all with them when they travel into remote parts, though still they take their weapons with them, for fear of thieves. Accordingly, there is, in every city where they live, one appointed particularly to take care of strangers, and to provide garments and other necessaries for them. But the habit and management of their bodies is such **as children** use who are in fear of their masters. Nor do they allow of the change of shoes till they be first torn to pieces, or worn out by time. Nor do they either buy or sell any thing to one another; but every one of them gives what he has to him that wants it, and receives from him again in lieu of it what may be convenient for himself; and although there be no requital made, they are fully allowed to take what they want of whomsoever they please.*

Philo of Alexandria: Hypothetica— Multitudes of his disciples has the lawgiver trained for the life of fellowship. These people are called Essenes, a name awarded to them doubtless in recognition of their holiness. They live in many cities of Judaea and in many villages and grouped in great societies of many members.

Josephus: The Jewish War, Book 2, Chapter 8, Paragraph 5 in part: [...] and if there be any strangers there, they sit down with them. Nor is there ever any clamor or disturbance to pollute their house, but they give every one leave to speak in their turn; which silence thus kept in their house appears to foreigners like some tremendous mystery; the cause of which is that perpetual sobriety they exercise, and the same settled measure of meat and drink that is allotted them, and that such as is abundantly sufficient for them.

The good soil to plant the seeds of thought into. Don't teach the "wise" old people Pharisees. Teach the children Essenes. Don't bother explaining any of this to church people. Share it with the homeless in the park.

Protected by the supernatural powers

*Lotus Sutra 14 - - - - - - - - When they preach this **Dharma** they will make no mistake [...] for this sutra is protected by the supernatural powers of all of the Buddhas of the past, present, and future.*

Matthew 10:19 But when they deliver you up, take no thought how or what ye shall speak: for it shall be given you in that same hour what ye shall speak.

Matthew 10:20 For it is not ye that speak, but the Spirit of your Father which speaketh in you.

*The words are not your own. They belong to the past and future Buddhas of every realm that can be imagined. You are tuned in and you resonate with the frequency of the **Dharma**.*

*It is the **Dharma** echoing in your mind that finds its way out in the words you select to convey the thoughts that the **Dharma** inspires you to contemplate. It speaks through you.*

Perseverance, with a gentle compliance, and with a non-violent disalarming mind

Lotus Sutra 14 - - - - - - - - *Take a stand on perseverance, with a gentle compliance, and with a non-violent disalarming mind.*

Matthew 10:22 And ye shall be hated of all men for my name's sake: but he that endureth to the end shall be saved.

This is key. Hang in there. Shout for peace. Scream over the noise of the war machine. Love, compassion, empathy, logic, sense, will outlast the hate and violence and selfishness.

All hidden will be revealed; all will be given Light; all will become Lights

Culahatthipadopama Sutta 27 - - - - - - - - *All fallen over will be set upright. All hidden will be revealed. All lost will find their way.* **All groping in the darkness will be given a lamp to hold up**.

Matthew 10:25-27 It is enough for the disciple that he be as his master, and the servant as his lord. If they have called the master of the house Beelzebub, how much more shall they call them of his household? Fear them not therefore: for there is nothing covered, that shall not be revealed; and hid, that shall not be known. What I tell you in darkness, that speak ye in light: and what ye hear in the ear, that preach ye upon the housetops.

This is one of those parallels that stand out due to the inclusion of specific terms in a specific order: covered, revealed, darkness, light. The Buddhist version predates the Gospel version by 600 years. The more of these that we collect and consider, the better the case is made for Buddhist missionary influence on the formation of the Gospel texts.

Beelzebub, Baal, is the god of alternative thought, villainized in Jewish scriptures. Different? You bet, and shout that from the rooftops while you're at it. Better than lurking around in underground tunnels waiting for Romans to pass by so you can attack them.

Kandaraka Sutta 13 - - - - - - - - *It is not easy to remain living at home and to lead the holy life utterly perfect and pure as a polished shell. Go forth from the home life into homelessness.* **Abandon your fortunes**. **Abandon your relatives**.

Lotus Sutra 01 - - - - - - - - *I see bodhisattvas (saints) who have given their very lives, their work and their community standing, have left behind wives and children, and followed the ultimate Way. I see bodhisattvas who would gladly put their head on the line, their eyes, life and limb, in exchange for the Buddha's* **Dharma**.

Cullavagga 9:1:4 - - - - - - - - *As the mighty rivers reach the sea, they* **lose their former individuality and become parts of the great ocean**, *so do disciples forsake their former families and* **nationalities** *and become part of Buddha's family.*

Matthew 10:37-38 : He that loveth father or mother more than me is not worthy of me: and he that loveth son or daughter more than me is not worthy of me.   And he that taketh not his cross, and followeth after me, is not worthy of me.

Matthew 16:24 Then said Jesus unto his disciples, If any man will come after me, let him deny himself, and take up his cross, and follow me.

Matthew 10:39 He that findeth his life shall lose it: and he that loseth his life for my sake shall find it.

Matthew 16:25 For whosoever will save his life shall lose it: and whosoever will lose his life for my sake shall find it.

From patriotism to cosmopolitan scope.   From assimilating the world into the rule of the Chosen to assimilating everyone into the Cosmopolitan scope of the Roman Empire.   From Simon being the Messiah Nasi to Hadrian being Caesar.

Take up your cross, pull out your stake, and follow the path away from all of the hopes for glory and conquest.   Leave it all behind, run away.   Such a call to flee all would only be this strong in the context of a very deadly war.   Cast your vote, War or Peace, and don't vote just because of the choices of your family, your connections, your stuff, your future.   Vote Peace because it means more to you than anything.   Vote Peace because you would rather have nothing than to share in the treasures of the end of a War that has cost so much to so many people, friend and enemy alike.   Pull up stake and let it go. Unplant your flag that claims your territory.

Worthy of gifts

Vatthupama Sutta 07 - - - - - - - - *The Sangha of the Blessed One's disciples is worthy of gifts, of hospitality, of offerings, of greetings of reverence—for they are* **the unsurpassed force of merit** *for the world.*

Akankheyya Sutta 05 - - - - - - - - *The offerings of those who give to one who fulfils the precepts give the giver great fruit and benefit— whether the gift is clothing, food, a place to sleep, or medicine.*

Lotus Sutra 28 - - - - - - - - *If there is anyone who offers alms to them and praises them, then in this present life there will be much blessing because of it.*

Matthew 10:40 : He that receiveth you receiveth me, and he that receiveth me receiveth him that sent me.

Matthew 10:42 And whosoever shall give to drink unto one of these little ones a cup of cold water [only] in the name of a disciple, verily I say unto you, he shall in no wise lose his reward.

Blind, deaf, dumb

Lalitavistra Sutra 7 - - - - - - - - *The **sick** are healed, the hungry and thirsty no longer know hunger and thirst, the addicts lose their addiction, the insane recover their sanity, the **blind** regain their sight, the **deaf** regain their hearing, the crippled and **lame** recover perfect limbs, the **poor** become rich, and the prisoners are set free.*

Jataka - - - - - - - - *Now the instant the Future Buddha was conceived in the womb of his mother, all the ten thousand worlds suddenly quaked, quivered, and shook. And the Thirty-two Prognostics appeared, as follows: an immeasurable light spread through ten thousand worlds; the **blind** recovered their sight, as if from desire to see this his glory; the **deaf** received their hearing; the dumb talked; the hunchbacked became straight of body; the **lame** recovered the power to walk; all those in bonds were freed from their bonds and chains; the fires went out in all the hells; the hunger and thirst of the Manes was stilled; wild animals lost their timidity; diseases ceased among men; all mortals became mild-spoken, horses neighed and elephants trumpeted in a manner sweet to the ear; all musical instruments gave forth their notes without being played upon; bracelets and other ornaments jingled; in all quarters of the heavens the weather became fair; a mild, cool breeze began to blow, very refreshing to men; rain fell out of season; water burst forth from the earth and flowed in streams; the birds ceased flying through the air; the rivers checked their flowing; in the mighty ocean the water became sweet; the ground became everywhere covered with lotuses of the five different colors; all flowers bloomed, both those on land and those that grow in the water; trunk-lotuses bloomed on the trunks of trees, branch-lotuses on the branches, and vine-lotuses on the vines; on the ground, stalk-lotuses, as they are called, burst through the overlying rocks and came up by sevens; in the sky were produced others, called hanging-lotuses; a shower of flowers fell all about; celestial music was heard to play in the sky; and the whole ten thousand worlds became one mass of garlands of the utmost possible magnificence, with waving chowries, and saturated with the incense-like fragrance of flowers, and resembled a bouquet of flowers sent whirling through the air, or a closely woven wreath, or a superbly decorated altar of flowers.*

Matthew 11:4-5 Jesus answered and said unto them, Go and shew John again those things which ye do hear and see: The blind receive their sight, and the lame walk, the lepers are cleansed, and the deaf hear, the dead are raised up, and the poor have the gospel preached to them.

The sick, the suffering internally, are given healing. The lepers, the suffering externally, are given cleansing. The dead, dead of body, are given reviving. The possessed, dead of mind, are given freeing. The poetic imagery of Mahayana is nice because it conveys this wonderful idea and at the same time lets your mind know it is not a literal or historical thing. It is a subjective truth.

Hearing

Ariyapariyesana Sutta 21 - - - - - - - - Open for them the gateway to immortality. **Let those who can hear realize their enlightenment.**

Bhaddali Sutta 32 - - - - - - - - Listen to the **Dharma** *with eager ears.*

Matthew 11:15 He that hath ears to hear, let him hear.

The catch phrase of find those who can listen and talk to them is repeated throughout Buddhist scriptures and is found in eight verses in the Gospels. If you can hear it, the song gets stuck in your head and plays itself back. It rocks you. It inspires you. Storytelling is cleansing, cathartic. The song gives you a voice to tell your story.

Kingdom within

*Satipatthanasamyutta 09; Mahaparinibbana Sutta 2:26 - - - - - - - - Dwell with yourself as **your own island**. Become for yourself **your own refuge**, with no other refuge. Dwell with this **Dharma** as your island. Have it become for you your own refuge, with no other refuge.*

*Ariyapariyesana Sutta 16 - - - - - - - - The **Dharma** that you enter into and make into your home is realized for yourself with **direct experience**.*

Luke 17:20-21 And when he was demanded of the Pharisees, when the kingdom of God should come, he answered them and said, The kingdom of God cometh not with observation: Neither shall they say, Lo here! Or, lo there! For, behold, the kingdom of God is within you.

My favorite Bible verse. When will Jesus fly out of the sky? He won't ever because he lives in your heart, not in outer space, silly!

Wisdom is purified by morality

Mahavedalla Sutta 11-12 - - - - - - - - You understand a state that can be known with the eye of wisdom. The purpose of wisdom is direct knowledge, full understanding, abandoning.

Sonadanda Sutta 22 - - - - - - - - Wisdom is purified by morality, and morality is purified by wisdom.

Matthew 11:19 The Son of man came eating and drinking, and they say, Behold a man gluttonous, and a winebibber, a friend of publicans and sinners. But wisdom is justified of her children.

Who is the simple man of Wisdom in a world gone mad with fears and violent intentions? The soldiers all prepare to engage in battle with great seriousness and discipline, short hair and uniform clothing. Who is the Hippie talking about Peace and Love? Just some civilian, just another consumer, another idiot who has the wrong politics (publican) and wrong religious (sinner) ideas. Ah, but which will Lady Wisdom be proud of in the end?

I am simple and poor

Tao Te Ching 20 - - - - - - - - **They are learned and proud.** *I am detached and hard to reach.* **They are sensible and prudent.** *I am neglected as a deaf-mute. They have collected their wealth. I am simple and poor. In the eyes of man, I am Poor and simple, but I have the food of Mother Way to nourish me.*

Matthew 11:25 At that time Jesus answered and said, I thank thee, O Father, Lord of heaven and earth, because thou hast hid these things from the wise and prudent, and hast revealed them unto babes.

The parallel of the terms wise and prudent in the same order is noteworthy here. The educated thinker leaders all agreed that Simon was indeed the Messiah. He got the party support. He got the popularity of the people. He made all the right speeches to unite most everyone to his cause. Where is your curriculum vitae? Why should your book be given any consideration at all? Who are you?

Burdens and bits

Khandhasamyutta 22 - - - - - - - - *What is the* **heavy burden** *to have to carry?   It is the craving that demands renewed existence, along with delight and lust.   It is searching for delight here and there. It is craving for sensual pleasures, craving for existence, craving for extermination.   This I call quite a heavy burden to have to carry.*

Bhaddali Sutta 33 - - - - - - - - *A thoroughbred colt gets used to* **wearing the bit,** *then the harness.   Once the colt is peaceful in this, the trainer teaches him to keep in step, to run in a circle, to gallop, to charge, to display royal qualities in the heritage of a horse fit for a king.   The fastest, most responsive, gentlest horse will be rewarded with rubbings and brushings.   Hear the* **Dharma** *with eager ears.*

Matthew 11:28-30   Come unto me, all ye that labour and are heavy laden, and I will give you rest.   Take my yoke upon you, and learn of me; for I am meek and lowly in heart: and ye shall find rest unto your souls.   For my yoke is easy, and my burden is light.

Heavy and light, loads and harnesses, being weighted down and being guided.   Are you a mule or a race horse?   Are you praying for whatever you currently want out of life, praying for health, and at last praying for death, having carried the weight of the world on your back for your entire burdened life?   You are a thoroughbred racehorse who needs to be taught how to run and jump and live up to your potential.   Stop letting them define you and control you.   Drop all the stuff they piled up on top of you and let it all go.   The burden of agenda.   It has to be this way.   This has to be there.   That has to go. Forget it all.   Jump the fence.

Words have weighed down

Devatasamyutta 61 - - - - - - - - Words have weighed down all that there is. Nothing extends its rule further than that of words. Words are the one thing that has everything under its control.

Matthew 12:37 For by thy words thou shalt be justified, and by thy words thou shalt be condemned.

Words can form mental traps. The words and phrases used to describe things, types of people, attitudes, most everything, carry with them meanings. They influence the way we think. People kill for what words may have been spoken. Simon Bar Kokhba killed his uncle, Rabbi Elazar Hamodai, for thinking he had spoken with the Romans. Jesus spoke the word and Lazarus (Elazar) came back to life.

Ignoring of all signs

Mahavedalla Sutta 27 - - - - - - - - *There are two conditions for the attainment of the signless deliverance of mind—the ignoring of all signs and the paying attention to the element beyond signs.*

Matthew 12:39-40 But he answered and said unto them, An evil and adulterous generation seeketh after a sign; and there shall no sign be given to it, but the sign of the prophet Jonas: For as Jonas was three days and three nights in the whale's belly; so shall the Son of man be three days and three nights in the heart of the earth.

Luke 11:30 For as Jonas was a sign unto the Ninevites, so shall also the Son of man be to this generation.

Notice that Luke does not relate the Jonah reference to the three days and three nights. The people of Nineveh took Jonah at his word as a prophet. This is how Jesus is portrayed here in Luke.

Three days and three nights. Modern Christianity relates this to Jesus crucified on a Friday afternoon and coming back to life on Sunday morning. One night short. What if the three days meant three summers and three nights meant three winters? 132 to 135 is three years. The death gives way to renewed life. The war ended. The destruction gives way to rebuilding. There was no magic sign to signal the end of the war. It just played itself out with enough sword killings and starvation and destruction that there was no one left to fight.

Getting beyond it all.

Bojjhangasamyutta 39 - - - - - - - - *There are huge trees with tiny seeds and huge bodies, encirclers of others trees. The trees they encircle become bent, twisted, and split. Some clansmen have left behind sensual pleasures and gone forth from the householder life into homelessness.* ***Those same sensual pleasures or others even worse than them*** *cause him to become bent, twisted, or split.*

Matthew 12:43-45 When the unclean spirit is gone out of a man, he walketh through dry places, seeking rest, and findeth none. Then he saith, I will return into my house from whence I came out; and when he is come, he findeth it empty, swept, and garnished. Then goeth he, and taketh with himself seven other spirits more wicked than himself, and they enter in and dwell there: and the last state of that man is worse than the first. Even so shall it be also unto this wicked generation.

If you free up a space by getting rid of an old habit, then do nothing to fill that space, it will just fill up with more bad habits. If you clear land, then do nothing to fill that space, wild vines will grow and take over. Entropy is the lesson here. It is not enough to prepare a place. Once prepared, the window of opportunity shouldn't be missed.

Don't fake letting it all go. Don't let their mindset suck you back in, wrap back around you and trap you. Your purpose is beyond them. Don't let them try to redefine you within their paradigm.

Faith is the seed; where to plant it

Payasi Sutta 31; Sotapattisamyutta 25 - - - - - - - - *A farmer went into the woods with a plough and seeds. The soil there had never been disturbed, with **tree roots and rocks**. The seeds were **broken**, rotten by exposure to the heat for a long time. The seeds were not placed very deeply into the ground. There was not much rain. Do you think the farmer's seeds will germinate, sprout and grow, giving him a large crop?*

Lotus Sutra 03 - - - - - - - - *Those with **shallow** understanding, wrapped up in the five desires, cannot comprehend it when they hear it. Do not preach to them. Such people will fail to have faith and will slander this sutra, quickly destroying **the seeds for becoming a Buddha in the world**.*

Kasibharadvaga Sutta 2 - - - - - - - - *Faith is the seed. Good works is the rain. Wisdom is the plough. Mind is the rein. The handle is the **Dharma**. Determination is the goad. Work is the ox. Ploughing destroys the weeds of illusion. **Harvest is the fruits of Nirvana**.*

Matthew 13:3-9 : And he spake many things unto them in parables, saying, Behold, a sower went forth to sow; And when he sowed, some seeds fell by the way side, and the fowls came and devoured them up: Some fell upon stony places, where they had not much earth: and forthwith they sprung up, because they had no deepness of earth: And when the sun was up, they were scorched; and because they had no root, they withered away. And some fell among thorns; and the thorns sprung up, and choked them: But other fell into good ground, and brought forth fruit, some an hundredfold, some sixtyfold, some thirtyfold. Who hath ears to hear, let him hear.

The parable of the sower has a lot of resonance with the Buddhist parables about the varying fates of planting seeds. Spread the gospel, the good news of the alternative way. Choose well where you spend your efforts.

Part of you can transcend

Sotapattisamyutta 21 - - - - - - - - *When a person's mind has been fortified over a long period of time with the nutriments of faith, virtue, learning, generosity, and wisdom—that mind goes upwards toward distinction. It is as if a man submerged a pot of oil into a deep pool of water and then breaks it. All of the shards and fragments of the pot will sink down, but the oil will rise to the top.*

John 5:24   Verily, verily, I say unto you, He that heareth my word, and believeth on him that sent me, hath everlasting life, and shall not come into condemnation; but is passed from death unto life.

The idea of ascending, arising, reaching out of the pit of hopelessness into a new beginning, born again unto a new possibility, is a concept that we find as a thread across several mystical paths. Rise above the ordinary. Break away from the herd. You are better than that.

Part of you cannot

Tao Te Ching 50 - - - - - - - - *Sprit transcends mortality.*

John 6:63   It is the spirit that quickeneth; the flesh profiteth nothing: the words that I speak unto you, they are spirit, and they are life.

Choose your audience wisely

*Canki Sutta 19-20 - - - - - - - - The **Dharma** cannot be easily taught by one affected by delusion. Once investigated and the states based on delusion having been eradicated, he gains a respect, he gives ear and listens to the **Dharma**, memorizing it, examining it, reflectively accepting it, springing up zeal for it, applying his will, scrutinizing, resolutely striving, and contractually experiencing the direct realization of the ultimate truth with a vision of penetrating wisdom.*

Matthew 13:19 When any one heareth the word of the kingdom, and understandeth it not, then cometh the wicked one, and catcheth away that which was sown in his heart. This is he which received seed by the way side.

*Blind faith in their bullshit causes the focus of **Gnosis** to be lost. The delusion has to be abandoned. Apostate from that blind faith. No more closed mindedness now that you are open to respecting foreign spiritual truths. At last, those who have lost their religion can begin their spiritual journey.*

Fruit grows into the most regal of trees

*Tathagatagarbha Sutra - - - - - - - - It is just like the pit of a mango fruit which does not decay. Plant it in the earth and inevitably a great tree grows. The Tathagata's faultless vision sees that the Tathagatagarbha within the bodies of sentient beings is just like the seed within a flower or fruit. Though ignorance covers the buddhagarbha, you ought to have faith and realize that you are possessed of Samadhi wisdom, none of which can be destroyed. for this reason, I expound the **Dharma** and reveal the Tathagatagarbha, that you may quickly attain the highest path, just as a fruit grows into the most regal of trees.*

Matthew 13:23 But he that received seed into the good ground is he that heareth the word, and understandeth it; which also beareth fruit, and bringeth forth, some an hundredfold, some sixty, some thirty.

We all have this sacred living core overgrown by the weeds of life. It will ultimately be all that matters. All of us. Everyone.

Safe and good path (the two influences)

*Dvedhavitakka Sutta 25 - - - - - - - - There was a wooded range with a low-lying marsh that was home to a large deer herd. **One man desired their ruin, harm, and capture**, so he closed the safe and good path that led to their happiness and opened up a replacement false path so that the deer might come upon calamity, disaster, loss. **Another man desired their good, welfare, protection**, so he reopened the safe and good path that led to their happiness and closed off the replacement false path, destroying the temptation. So the large herd of deer proceeded to growth, increase, and fulfillment.*

Matthew 13:24-30   Another parable put he forth unto them, saying, The kingdom of heaven is likened unto a man which sowed good seed in his field: But while men slept, his enemy came and sowed tares among the wheat, and went his way. But when the blade was sprung up, and brought forth fruit, then appeared the tares also. So the servants of the householder came and said unto him, Sir, didst not thou sow good seed in thy field? From whence then hath it tares? He said unto them, An enemy hath done this. The servants said unto him, Wilt thou then that we go and gather them up? But he said, Nay; lest while ye gather up the tares, ye root up also the wheat with them. Let both grow together until the harvest: and in the time of harvest I will say to the reapers, Gather ye together first the tares, and bind them in bundles to burn them: but gather the wheat into my barn.

Calamity, disaster, loss – words describing war – conflict, revolution, terrorist activity. The path of war. The seeds of choking ideas, fears, anger, violence, division, hatred, relentless determination. Once the fruit of the bad seeds are taken out of the equation, the resulting harvest is one of purity. The meek inherit the earth after the violent are all dead and gone. Good seeds, bad seeds, is not so much different people as it is different aspects of each of us. Good views and bad views, good intentions and bad intentions, good words and bad words, good actions and bad actions. A good housecleaning of the garden of the mind and we can burn away the weeds and let our harvest be more valuable, more pure.

Because of the soil

Maggasamyutta 150 - - - - - - - - *Whatever types of seeds are planted have their growth, increase, and expansion because of the soil, established in the soil. Planted in virtue, established in virtue, a bhikkhu develops and cultivates the Noble Eightfold Path and by doing so attains* **growth, increase, and expansion in wholesome states**.

Mark 4:26-29 And he said, So is the kingdom of God, as if a man should cast seed into the ground; And should sleep, and rise night and day, and the seed should spring and grow up, he knoweth not how. For the earth bringeth forth fruit of herself; first the blade, then the ear, after that the full corn in the ear. But when the fruit is brought forth, immediately he putteth in the sickle, because the harvest is come.

Mark preserves this gem that is somehow lost to Matthew. Once the seed is planted correctly in fertile soil, it can only grow. Growth is its nature. Those who get it are transformed by it. You don't have to understand it or even have faith in it, you just have to let it happen.

Tiny twig

Tao Te Ching 64 - - - - - - - - *A tree that it takes both arms to encircle was **once a tiny twig**.*

Matthew 13:31-32 Another parable put he forth unto them, saying, The kingdom of heaven is like to a grain of mustard seed, which a man took, and sowed in his field: Which indeed is the least of all seeds: but when it is grown, it is the greatest among herbs, and becometh a tree, so that the birds of the air come and lodge in the branches thereof.

Similes

Payasi Sutta 09; Rathavinita Sutta 14 - - - - - - - - I will give you similes, for some who are wise can grasp the meaning conveyed by means of a simile.

*Lotus Sutra 02 - - - - - - - - When the hearers and bodhisattvas listen to the **Dharma** that I preach, as soon as they have grasped one sentence, they will without a doubt be assured of attaining Buddhahood.*

Lotus Sutra 03 - - - - - - - - I expressly command you to not preach this sutra to those who are unwise.

Matthew 13:10-13 And the disciples came, and said unto him, Why speakest thou unto them in parables? He answered and said unto them, Because it is given unto you to know the mysteries of the kingdom of heaven, but to them it is not given. For whosoever hath, to him shall be given, and he shall have more abundance: but whosoever hath not, from him shall be taken away even that he hath. Therefore speak I to them in parables: because they seeing see not; and hearing they hear not, neither do they understand.

Matthew 13:34 All these things spake Jesus unto the multitude in parables; and without a parable spake he not unto them:

*Contractually experiencing the direct realization of the ultimate truth with a vision of penetrating wisdom is lost on an audience of people bent on war and conquest and riches. The secrets of the kingdom of heaven are like the war plans of the conquest of earth, to be known only to those dedicated and participating in the effort. You don't publish your battle plans for everyone to see. The **Dharma** is the plan for attaining and obtaining the kingdom not of this world. It is only for the recruits.*

You only get stories, hints, mysteries. Similes, parables, fables, riddles, legends, characters, fantasies, patterns of ideas, dreams. You don't get real. People get hung up on pure logic, rational arguments, reasoning, being pre-programmed with a counter-response, a shut-down mechanism for keeping strong the fields of prejudice, of allegiance to political and religious ideas, of assumptions and limitations. Fiction allows for the silencing of the logical feedback circuit, for it is only a cartoon, it is only a story, it is only make believe. From Aesop's Fables through the Brothers Grimm to Walt

*Disney, stories were used to present ideas not easily spoken of in a direct manner. Science fiction has served in modern times to explore the differences in peoples as presented in the stories about differences in alien beings. Stories are not facts, not historical, not literally true. You can't go back in time and space and witness the events in person. They exist only in mindscape. Subjective truth, living **Dharma**. You can use these as a framework, as a platform, as a way of remembering. The story is true even though it never actually happened. It is within this world of parables that Jesus teaches. It is within this world of parables that Jesus lives.*

There are not too many parables in Jewish literature, while Buddhist teachings are filled with such stories. That Jesus is teaching parables instead of reciting from the 613 laws of Moses is an important observation. We have a lot to ponder about the stories preserved: how they relate to similar Buddhist stories, what they would have meant in the context of Jewish rebellion against Roman rule, and what they as a group add up to in conveying the purpose and direction of the early Jesus stories.

Another consideration is that while it is obvious that the stories that Jesus tells are parables and the characters are not meant to be taken as historical and the events are not eye witness accounts, we could make the same conclusions regarding the stories about Jesus. Then we would have events like the walking on the water and the feeding of the 5000 as being parables and not histories.

Priceless gem hidden in his garment

Surangama Sutra - - - - - - - - Sentient beings are like a man with a priceless gem hidden in his garment of which he is ignorant. He becomes poor and ragged and hungry and wanders about to distant lands. Although he is actually suffering from poverty, he still is in possession of the priceless gem. One day a very wise man tells the poor man of his priceless gem and from that time the poor man becomes very wealthy.

Tathagatagarbha Sutra - - - - - - - - It is like a traveler to another country carrying a golden statue, who wraps it in dirty, worn-out rags and discards it in an unused field. One with supernatural vision sees it and tells other people about it. They remove the dirty rags and reveal the statue and all rejoice greatly. My supernatural vision is like this. I see that beings of all sorts are entangled in klesas and evil actions and are plagued with all the sufferings of samsara. Yet I also see that within the dust of ignorance of all beings, the Tathagata nature sits motionless, great and indestructible. After I have seen this, I explain to bodhisattvas that klesas and evil actions cover the most victorious body. You should endeavor to sever them, and manifest the Tathagata wisdom. It is the refuge of all gods, men, nagas, and spirits.

Matthew 13:44 Again, the kingdom of heaven is like unto treasure hid in a field; the which when a man hath found, he hideth, and for joy thereof goeth and selleth all that he hath, and buyeth that field.

Planted, buried, hidden, secret, you can know what is not obvious to others. You can discover what is not obvious to yourself.

False home: his own father's house

Ratthapala Sutta 17 - - - - - - - - *Ratthapala the venerable holy man went to his own father's house and he received there neither alms nor polite words, but rather only abuse.*

Matthew 13:57 And they were offended in him. But Jesus said unto them, A prophet is not without honour, save in his own country, and in his own house.

I'm supposed to insert snide remarks about my family not understanding me, not accepting me, wanting to save me and make me one of them instead. Pass.

Two different disciples

*Dhammadayada Sutta 3 - - - - - - - - The Blessed One left behind some food one evening. One disciple remembered the lesson to treasure the **Dharma** and not the material and passed by the food, remaining hungry and weak for the night and the following day. Another disciple ate the leftover food, being full for the night and the following day. The Blessed One commented: Blessed is the disciple who has passed by the food. He has learned the lesson of how to be satisfied with few concerns, contented, not selfish, easily maintained, and in control of his desires. Out of compassion for you I have taught you to be my heirs in the **Dharma** and not the material.*

Luke 10:38-42 Now it came to pass, as they went, that he entered into a certain village: and a certain woman named Martha received him into her house. And she had a sister called Mary, which also sat at Jesus' feet, and heard his word. But Martha was cumbered about much serving, and came to him, and said, Lord, dost thou not care that my sister hath left me to serve alone? bid her therefore that she help me. And Jesus answered and said unto her, Martha, Martha, thou art careful and troubled about many things: But one thing is needful: and Mary hath chosen that good part, which shall not be taken away from her.

The busy distracted mind is compared with the simple focused mind. The mind thrown into work and concerns about what needs to be accomplished, what opportunities arise, the logical traps of expectations and responsibilities, is caught in a web. The escape is simple. Let it all go. Don't let the center of your way of thinking become the being troubled about the encumbrances you have wrapped around yourself. We build our own traps and willingly sit in them.

True home: detached from the disturbances

Mahapadana Sutta 2:17 - - - - - - - - *It is not proper for me to live with a crowd like this. I must live **alone, withdrawn** from this crowd.*

Khandhasamyutta 81 - - - - - - - - *Without informing his closest companions, without dismissing the bhikkhu Sangha, he set out on a **solitary** journey without a companion.*

Maha-Assapura Sutta 12; Kandaraka Sutta 18 - - - - - - - - *Resort to a secluded resting place, the woods, underneath a tree, on a **secluded mountain**, a ravine, a cave on the side of a hill, a graveyard, the thicket of a jungle, an open field, or a heap of straw.*

Culasunnata Sutta 4 - - - - - - - - *Entering the forest, you gain confidence, steadiness, decision, **detached from the disturbances of the village** and the encountering of people there.*

Dhammadayada Sutta 6 - - - - - - - - *The disciples of the Teacher who live in seclusion are failing to train in seclusion, in not abandoning what the Teacher has taught them to abandon. They care for luxuries, leading the way to backsliding, neglectful of seclusion.*

Luke 4:42 And when it was day, he departed and went into a desert place: and the people sought him, and came unto him, and stayed him, that he should not depart from them.

Matthew 14:23 And when he had sent the multitudes away, he went up into a mountain apart to pray: and when the evening was come, he was there alone.

Thomas 49 Blessed are the solitary and elect, for you will find the kingdom. For you are from it, and to it you will return.

The inspiration of Jesus was not out of the traditions and culture of the Jewish people, but was seen as something alien, something received once distanced from the people. A mountain apart from all of that, secluded, solitary, undisturbed. You belong to the Dharma and she is calling you home, pulling you away from all of the distractions and disturbances. What did you go into the wilderness to see? You have to remember.

What do you get out away from everything, way past the limits of paved roads, Wi-Fi and telephone signals, people? No property lines, no ownership, nothing to spend money on, the term "value" takes on a different meaning. There are no words to be read, no words to be spoken, no one to talk to, no arguments, no competition, no rejection, no laws, no harassments, no judgments, no wars, no divisions, no agendas, no deadlines, no expectations, no responsibilities, no demands.

Walks on the water

Mahaparinibbana Sutta 1:33 - - - - - - - - *The Lord, as swiftly as a strong man might stretch out his flexed arm or flex it again, vanished from this side of the Ganges and reappeared with his order of monks on the other shore.*

Mahavagga 1:20:16 - - - - - - - - *At that time a great rain fell out of season; and a great inundation arose. The place where the Blessed One lived was covered with water. Then the Blessed One thought: 'What if I were to cause the water to recede round about, and if I were to walk up and down in the midst of the water on a dust-covered spot.' And the Blessed One caused the water to recede round about, and he walked up and down in the midst of the water on a dust-covered spot. And the Gatila Uruvela Kassapa, who was afraid that the water might have carried away the great Samana, went with a boat together with many Gatilas to the place where the Blessed One lived. Then the Gatila Uruvela Kassapa saw the Blessed One, who had caused the water to recede round about, walking up and down in the midst of the water on a dust-covered spot. Seeing him, he said to the Blessed One: 'Are you there, great Samana?'*

Anguttara Nikaya 3:60 - - - - - - - - *He walks on the water without making waves, as if on solid ground.*

Matthew 14:25 And in the fourth watch of the night Jesus went unto them, walking on the sea.

Jataka 190 - - - - - - - - *"Behold the fruit of sacrifice," etc.--This story the Master told whilst staying in Jetavana, about a believing layman. This was a faithful, pious soul, an elect disciple. One evening, on his way to Jetavana, he came to the bank of the river Aciravati, when the ferrymen had pulled up their boat on the shore in order to attend service; as no boat could be seen at the landing-stage, and our friend's mind being full of delightful thoughts of the Buddha, he walked into the river. His feet did not sink below the water. He got as far as mid-river walking as though he were on dry land; but there he noticed the waves. Then his ecstasy subsided, and his feet began to sink. Again he strung himself up to high tension, and walked on over the water. So he arrived at Jetavana, greeted the Master, and took a seat on one side. The Master entered into conversation with him pleasantly. "I hope, good layman," said he, "you had no mishap on your way." "Oh, Sir," he replied, "on my way I was so absorbed in thoughts of the Buddha that I set foot upon the river; but I walked over it as though it had been dry ground!" "Ah, friend layman," said the Master, "you are not the only one who has kept safe by remembering the virtues of the Buddha. In olden days pious laymen have been shipwrecked in mid-ocean, and saved themselves by remembering the Buddha's virtues."*

Akankheyya Sutta 14 - - - - - - - - Anyone who fulfils the precepts may wish to walk on water without sinking as though it was earth and such a supernatural power may be held.

Matthew 14:29 And he said, Come. And when Peter was come down out of the ship, he walked on the water, to go to Jesus.

Peter, the name literally means "rock", and there he is floating on top of the water. Impossible, at yet the imagined vision of this gives us hope. Subconsciousness hovers over the logical mind. The sea contains, defines, limits. The sea pushes you along with its currents. The storm, the wind, the sinking feeling, are all in the mind. There is a part of you hovering above it, putting it all underfoot and walking all over it.

Storm will end

Lotus Sutra 25 - - - - - - - - *If clouds should thunder and lightning and hail and rain, think of the power of that Hearer of Sounds and at that moment the storm will end.*

Matthew 14:32 And when they were come into the ship, the wind ceased.

Situations arise where there is an experience of a lack of control that resolve into peace. For all the feelings of sinking and being caught in a storm and being helpless go away.

Blind men clinging onto one another

Tevijja Sutta 15 - - - - - - - - *When the Brahmins learned in the three Vedas (Hindu Scriptures) teach a path that they do not know and have never seen, saying that this is the Only Way, they cannot possibly be correct. They are just as a line of blind men clinging onto one another, the first one sees nothing, the middle one sees nothing, and the last one sees nothing. They turn out to be laughable with their words empty and vain.*

Sallekha Sutta 16 - - - - - - - - *It is impossible for you to be sinking in the mud and to then pull out another person who is **sinking in the mud**.*

Lotus Sutra 02 - - - - - - - - *Having generated such volitional formations, they tumble down the slope of birth, tumble down the slope of growing old, **tumble down the slope** of death, and tumble down the slope of sorrow, lamentation, pain, displeasure, and despair.*

Matthew 15:14 Let them [alone]: they be blind leaders [of the blind]. And if the blind lead the blind, both shall fall into the ditch.

Matthew 23:24 Ye blind guides, which strain at a gnat, and swallow a camel.

The blind leading the blind famous quote from Jesus goes back 600 years before to Buddha. How many Bible thumpers does it take to understand the Big Bang Theory and Evolution? How many suicide bombers does it take to understand that Allah is not going to award them with virgins? You can be an outsider and look at some rich evangelical church drawing in thousands of people who sing along and write checks and buy into the whole show, and you wonder why they would fall for that? It is somehow human nature to follow leaders and to expect someone to show the way. But when you look closely, they are incompetent idiots. They quibble about the least detail of the matters, the little gnat bugs of life. Then they take a thick camel hair rope down the throat without even gagging on it.

You can't keep on taking advice from the same old set of idiots that put you in this mess in the first place.

Not the eating of food

Sutta Nipata 242 - - - - - - - - *Stealing, lying, and adultery—these defile, but not the eating of food.*

Matthew 15:17-20 Do not ye yet understand, that whatsoever entereth in at the mouth goeth into the belly, and is cast out into the draught? But those things which proceed out of the mouth come forth from the heart; and they defile the man. For out of the heart proceed evil thoughts, murders, adulteries, fornications, thefts, false witness, blasphemies: These are the things which defile a man: but to eat with unwashen hands defileth not a man.

A lot of religious identification and superstition revolves around diet. What is kosher? Jews and Muslims do not eat pork. Hindus do not eat beef. Many Buddhists are vegetarian. Jesus is given a rather humorous answer, though typically obscured by the translation. Whatever you put into your mouth ends up becoming shit. What you really need to watch out for is the shit coming out of your mouth.

Forget pop religion. It is a distraction, not a solution.

Your money or your life

Tao Te Ching 44 - - - - - - - - *Which is more valuable—your soul or your wealth? You should seek that which you treasure, being very careful to treasure the right things.*

Matthew 16:26 For what is a man profited, if he shall gain the whole world, and lose his own soul? Or what shall a man give in exchange for his soul?

What if you win the war? What if you defeat the arch nemesis and become the hero of the day? If the Promised Land comes at such a cost, what does that do to the soul of the Chosen People? Is it sometimes better to walk away with self-respect and dignity than to win the battle? Could something be treasured more so than actually winning?

Enlightened: transfiguration

Lotus Sutra 17 - - - - - - - - *In the depths of heart, believe and know and* **you will see the Buddha forever living on Mount Gridhrakuta**, *with the great bodhisattvas (saints) and multitude of those who hear his voice surrounding him as he preaches the* **Dharma** *(Kingdom).*

Mahaparinibbana Sutta 4:37 - - - - - - - - *It is wonderful, Lord, it is marvelous* **how clear and bright the Lord's skin appears**! *It looks even brighter than the golden robes in which it is clothed.*

Surangama Sutra - - - - - - - - *From the Lord's crown radiated outwardly* **countless beams of light**, *shooting out in all directions. In each of the bright beams there were intricate designs of transcendentally mysterious beings.*

Matthew 17:2 And was transfigured before them: and his face did shine as the sun, and his raiment was white as the light.

The vision of the glowing man transformed into light links the transfiguration story about Jesus with that of Buddha.

Imaginative

Anguttara Nikaya 6:24 - - - - - - - - *A monk advanced in concentration can split the Himalayas in two.*

Matthew 17:20 And Jesus said unto them, Because of your unbelief: for verily I say unto you, If ye have faith as a grain of mustard seed, ye shall say unto this mountain, Remove hence to yonder place; and it shall remove; and nothing shall be impossible unto you.

*You can imagine the impossible, even when you know it is impossible. You can see the potential for a tree when holding a tiny seed in your hand. You can see the impossible mountain in your face, the great war, and you can imagine it away. You plant the seed and have faith that it knows how to grow. You spread the **Dharma** about peace and love and you may not think it can take on that big mountain of bigotry and hate and fear, but you have to have the same faith that you would have when you plant a seed for a tree to grow.*

Innocent

*Tao Te Ching 10 - - - - - - - - Preserving humility and the **calm breathing of non-aggression**, you become like a little child.*

*Tao Te Ching 28 - - - - - - - - Realize the foolishness of angered response, keeping the mind one in **tranquility with the simplicity of a child**, conserving the spirit.*

*Tao Te Ching 55 - - - - - - - - A baby is weak of bones and muscles, but is spiritually pure. A child's **unity is unbroken**. To know the continuation of this unity and wholeness, you must return to the original state of simplicity. That which is fully-grown is in the process of decaying.*

Matthew 18:3-4 And said, Verily I say unto you, Except ye be converted, and become as little children, ye shall not enter into the kingdom of heaven. Whosoever therefore shall humble himself as this little child, the same is greatest in the kingdom of heaven.

Vulnerable

Lotus Sutra 10 - - - - - - - - If a bad person, completely lacking in goodness, should for an aeon stand before the Buddha and continuously curse and taunt him, that person's offense would be light compared to the person who speaks one harsh word to curse or belittle the disciple who reads and recites the Lotus Sutra.

Matthew 18:6-7 But whoso shall offend one of these little ones which believe in me, it were better for him that a millstone were hanged about his neck, and that he were drowned in the depth of the sea. Woe unto the world because of offences! For it must needs be that offences come; but woe to that man by whom the offence cometh!

Such a very specific clause to add to the Gospel that finds this parallel in the Lotus Sutra, a Mahayana Buddhist text current in time with that of the origin of the Jesus stories. That there is a magical curse on anyone who challenges the weak and vulnerable disciples before they are strong enough to grow in faith.

Professional theologians keep it complicated so they can pride themselves on being experts. Simplicity gets disrespected. Thinking cannot appreciate feelings. Logic cannot explain art. It is like they have a heavy stone sinking them down into the sea that Jesus is walking above.

The rules of life

Sallekha Sutta 12 - - - - - - - - Do not be cruel. Do not kill living beings. Do not take what is not given to you. Do not concern yourself with sexual conquests. Do not speak false words. Do not speak maliciously. Do not speak harshly. Do not gossip. Do not covet. Do not hold to ill will. Do not hold to wrong views. Do not hold to wrong intentions. Do not hold to wrong speech. Do not hold to wrong action. Do not keep a bad job. Do not continue in wrong effort. Do not continue in wrong mindfulness. Do not continue in wrong concentration. Do not continue in wrong knowledge. Do not continue in wrong deliverance. Do not be overcome by laziness and inactivity. Do not be restless. Do not be doubtful. Do not be angry. Do not be revengeful. Do not be contemptuous. Do not be domineering. Do not be envious. Do not be greedy. Do not be fraudulent. Do not be deceitful. Do not be stubborn. Do not be arrogant. Do not be difficult to admonish. Do not keep bad friends. Do not be negligent. Do not be faithless. Do not be shameless. Do not abandon fear of wrongdoing. Do not be shallow in thinking. Do not be lazy. Do not be unmindful. Do not be lacking in wisdom. Do not be stubborn in clinging to views.

Matthew 19:17-18 And he said unto him, Why callest thou me good? There is none good but one, [that is, God]: but if thou wilt enter into life, keep the commandments. He saith unto him, Which? Jesus said, Thou shalt do no murder, Thou shalt not commit adultery, Thou shalt not steal, Thou shalt not bear false witness,

The "Law" according to Buddha, all without the penalties of death for non-compliance. Timeless truths can be appreciated by all. Search the Empire and collect the best ideas into one cosmopolitan state law.

There is none good but one. Someone added in the words "that is, God" into this verse. It is not found in the originals. We could see it as a reference to Buddha, the one who perfected Right Actions as part of his Noble Eightfold Path. Through the lens of Christianity linking Jesus to the Jewish scriptures, we would assume he is referring to the Law of Moses here. This Buddhist scripture reference offers an alternative for our consideration.

No distinction

Diamond Sutra 23 - - - - - - - - Consider no distinction between yourself and the selfhood of others. Practice charity by giving not just tangible gifts, but also the selfless gifts of kindness and charity.

Matthew 19:19 Honour thy father and thy mother: and, Thou shalt love thy neighbour as thyself.

No seniority

Sotapattisamyutta 54 - - - - - - - - *I see no difference between a disciple who has just attained liberation in mind and a bhikkhu who has been liberated in mind for a hundred years. One's liberation is the same as that of the other.*

Matthew 20:12-16 Saying, These last have wrought but one hour, and thou hast made them equal unto us, which have borne the burden and heat of the day. But he answered one of them, and said, Friend, I do thee no wrong: didst not thou agree with me for a penny? Take that thine is, and go thy way: I will give unto this last, even as unto thee. Is it not lawful for me to do what I will with mine own? Is thine eye evil, because I am good? So the last shall be first, and the first last: [for many be called, but few chosen].

*From priest to bishop to pope, organized religion has a structure, a ranking. **Dharma** is flat, sharing, willing to teach but just as eager to learn, grown but ready to fully evolve. This is a different mindset where what is valued are those practical ideas more so than the prestige and seniority of the speaker of the ideas.*

Not participating in their religion; a sacrifice at which no oxen are slain

Payasi Sutta 31 - - - - - - - - *At a **sacrifice at which no oxen are slain**, nor goats, birds, pigs, nor any other animal, but where the people there have the right view, the right thought, the right speech, the right action, the right livelihood, the right effort, the right mindfulness, and the right concentration, then the sacrifice is of plentiful fruit and profit, shining with a majestic Light.*

Matthew 21:12   And Jesus went into the temple [of God], and cast out all them that sold and bought in the temple, and overthrew the tables of the moneychangers, and the seats of them that sold doves,

Christian theologians read Jesus disrupting the flow of people wanting to sacrifice animals in the Temple as being because he thought they were being greedy or the system was corrupt or some other explanation. From a Buddhist perspective, or Pythagorean for that matter, the objection would be to the very concept of killing animals being equated with the making of spiritual progress. The message was clearly to stop participating in the old religion and start performing spiritual rituals that will actually make a difference. If you want to kill something, kill ignorance, malice, harsh words, violence, war, blind patriotism, blind faith, and having such a limited self-identity as to want to perpetuate such an archaic system of thought.

Epiphanius noted that in the Ebionite gospel Jesus says, "I am come to do away with sacrifices, and if ye cease not from sacrificing, the wrath of God will not cease from you."

*The explanation that he was only concerned with the money involved doesn't seem to fully explain the situation. His answer that follows in the gospel texts is that this Temple won't last but the Temple of his body will live forever. What may should be obvious, but is not due to Christian theology getting in the way, is that the body of Christ that is the eternal Temple is none other than the disciples who live for the **Dharma**. They are the community that presents itself as a living sacrifice. This is the vision of Jesus for his Church, for his body. The body is the Church, the Sangha. In Buddhism there are* *three jewels – the Buddha, the **Dharma**, and the Sangha. It could be thought of in Christian terms – the Christ, the Gospel, and the Church. The purpose of the Church is to continue the **Dharma**, the Gospel, of the Christ, to be its body.*

It was already considered a century before the Gospel text was composed that it is time for religion to evolve beyond the animal sacrifice primitiveness. What does it mean to offer a sacredness instead of an animal? Beyond Bronze Age spirituality. Evolving.

Anyone who completely follows the Law without deviating will be accepted by God as an offering of an atoning sacrifice and be accepted into the New Testament of the Eternal Yahad (Solidarity). [Dead Sea Scrolls 1QS 3:10-12]

Guided by the instruction of the Holy Spirit, they shall become an atonement for the guilt of transgression. For the rebellion of sin, they shall become an acceptable sacrifice for the land, just as the burnt offerings. Prayer shall become the very means for grace to be attained, the sweet odor of righteous and holy lives will be considered to be a pleasing freewill offering. [Dead Sea Scrolls 1QS 9:4-5]

No untimely blossoms

Mahaparinibbana Sutta 5:2 - - - - - - - - Those twin sal-trees burst into an abundance of untimely blossoms.

Matthew 21:18-19 Now in the morning as he returned into the city, he hungered. And when he saw a fig tree in the way, he came to it, and found nothing thereon, but leaves only, and said unto it, Let no fruit grow on thee henceforward for ever. And presently the fig tree withered away.

Mark 11:13 And seeing a fig tree afar off having leaves, he came, if haply he might find any thing thereon: and when he came to it, he found nothing but leaves; for the time of figs was not yet.

Sometimes you expect things to be different, to jump out of season to line up for you and support you. It is obvious in this parable that the fruitless tree that withers and dies forever symbolized the Chosen People, the Israelites, the Messianic Jews, those rallied around Simon in hopes that God will give them their Promised Land. There was such a potential with the heritage of these people, one of the first with a written alphabet, collections of wisdom literature, positioned to become such an inspiration for the world, but such fruits were not to be seen. With great potential comes great responsibility and expectations, to bloom, to produce fruit, to give happiness to those around. Instead, it produced terrorism.

Run up and down along the bank

Maggasamyutta 034 - - - - - - - - *Few are those among humanity who go beyond to the far shore. Most people merely run up and down along the bank.*

Matthew 22:14 For many are called, but few are chosen.

*The few have a different defined quantity of value, of what it means to be successful, of what it means to reach their goal in life. The rat race of the world is keeping people running back and forth to respond to every call, every new trend, every collective idea of what they are supposed to care about and want, how they are supposed to talk about things, what they are supposed to be doing, playing their part in a time-wasting game that leads them to nowhere. There is a difference in the many and the few, the common herd and the lone wolves. The few can tune out all of the background noise and select the Path that advances them. Instead of pacing back and forth with the mindless on the near shore of life, the few build a raft and cross the stream and stand on that distant shore in the mind from which they can look back at the rest of humanity lost in their rat races and getting nowhere. **Dharma** is the raft.*

Given up the use of gold and silver

Gamanisamyutta 10 - - - - - - - - *The ascetics following the Sakyan son do not accept gold and silver. They renounce jewelry and gold. They have given up the use of gold and silver.*

Matthew 22:19-21 Shew me the tribute money. And they brought unto him a penny. And he saith unto them, Whose is this image and superscription? They say unto him, Caesar's. Then saith he unto them, Render therefore unto Caesar the things which are Caesar's; and unto God the things that are God's.

Thomas 100 They showed Jesus a gold coin and said to him, "The Roman emperor's people demand taxes from us." He said to them, "Give the emperor what belongs to the emperor, give God what belongs to God, and give me what is mine."

They're coming to take your stuff, let them have it. They're coming to sit in your seat, time to move along anyway. Give to politics what politics says you owe to it. Give to religion what religion says you owe to it. Not of that belongs to me. None of that is who I really am. As long as you are a this or a that, you have to stand up for this, stand up against that, be patriotic, have faith, play your role as slaves to their sense of value.

When Simon took control of Jerusalem in 132, he declared it to be "year one" and had coins made up to be used instead of the Roman money. This was the only historical reference in the Roman Empire years of Jerusalem to there being coins that you would have to look at to see if they belonged to Caesar (Roman money) or to God (Simon money). There are coins from the Kusan Empire with a Hellenistic style picture of Buddha and the Greek word "Boddo" dated to around the year 120. Whose coins are you carrying?

Respect of others

Surangama Sutra - - - - - - - - *They want the respect of others, wanting to be seen as superior, greedily watching over the offerings of the people.*

Labhasakkarasamyutta 10 - - - - - - - - *You who are overcome and obsessed with wanting to be praised will be reborn in a state of disgrace.*

Matthew 23:6-7 And love the uppermost rooms at feasts, and the chief seats in the synagogues, And greetings in the markets, and to be called of men, Rabbi, Rabbi.

Luke 6:26 Woe unto you, when all men shall speak well of you! For so did their fathers to the false prophets.

Who is an important expert deserving respect, superior to the common way that people think, praised as being a prophet who speaks for God? When those who say they are experts are recommending violence as the direction, holy wars, crusades, and they get the respect and cooperation of the people, the result is never good. The idea of "false prophets" perverting otherwise good traditions is brought up here. Who are the false prophets that the fathers of Judaism spoke well of? The writings of the prophets collected in the Bible? The prophecies for a great Messiah to come and for the whole world to fall in surrender to God being on his side? The Samaritans (Ebionites) rejected the collection of the Jewish Prophets. The Samaritans cooperated with the Romans, considered that their God of the Mountain was the same as the Jupiter that the Romans so admired, the Zeus of the Greeks. The Jews were led by experts on Messianic prophecies who concluded that Simon was indeed backed by God and would defeat the Romans and that every Jew should respect their understanding and back up this Messiah in his holy war effort.

Those who seem right are wrong. Unlearn your faith in them. You aren't qualified to have an opinion according to them. Your new insights are alien within the context of their assumptions.

Cold Reception

Lotus Sutra 02 - - - - - - - - *The appearance of a Buddha in the world is rare and difficult to take place. When they do appear, it is often difficult for them to preach the* **Dharma***.*

John 1:11   He came unto his own, and his own received him not.

The Answer is rejected by those who think they have it all figured out and dare not question their accepted conclusions. When the people are rallying for revolution, talks of peace with those vastly different come across as being unpatriotic, unfaithful. The **Dharma** *is bigger than the sand castles of small minds, bigger than the ivory towers of those who proclaim themselves experts, and bigger than the "house of cards" so-called reality that most people imagine to be true. Those living in the matrix think those who see the reality beyond the matrix must be insane. It is beyond a small paradigm shift to prepare to meet the Buddha, to meet the Jesus, to escape the mind games and at last awaken.*

Jesus, a concept of "Salvation" incarnate dreamed up by ancient Jewish minds, the ultimate Joshua (Jesus) to lead us to the ultimate promised land inheritance, is lost on the world of Messianic Judaism. Its Messiah (Christ) was one of war and conquest of earthly territories. The Jesus of the Gospel was a bringer of "Salvation" in a different way, promising a conquered kingdom not of this world, a spiritual connection and perfection that is beyond the traditional religious definitions and understandings, and as such this Jesus was less suited for inspiring Messianic Jews than for holistic spiritual seekers across the Roman Empire.

Anguttara Nikaya 7:68 - - - - - - - - - *Sixty more gave up the discipline and returned to the lower realms of being. Difficult is the path of the resurrected.*

John 6:66-67   From that time many of his disciples went back, and walked no more with him. Then said Jesus unto the twelve, Will ye also go away?

This is not for everyone. Everyone is not ready for it. It is a different way of thinking, a different life, a different outlook, a different self-identity, a different set of values. Can you imagine following the Buddha and the people around you don't appreciate him and leave? Can you imagine following Jesus and the people around you don't appreciate him and leave? It is like that. So if people don't understand you and don't respect that you are onto something real here, you are in good company.

No one as your spiritual father

Tao Te Ching 04 - - - - - - - - *Recognize no one as your spiritual father, for no one is worthy to be known as our ancestor except the Perfect Father.*

Tao Te Ching 08 - - - - - - - - **Be like water**, *choosing the lowest place, being of the greatest use, being kind and courteous, resonating with the good in others, speaking only true and kind words, seeking peace and order, striving to do your best, and being willing to yield to change.*

Matthew 23:8-10 But be not ye called Rabbi: for one is your Master, [even Christ]; and all ye are brethren. And call no man your father upon the earth: for one is your Father, which is in heaven. Neither be ye called masters: for one is your Master, even Christ.

*Fire climbs up. Water seeps down. Fire consumes. Water fills. Fire has to act fast, has to find others to fuel the burn, for with all of its energy it is fleeting, the bright Nasi of the moment, and the whole timeless array of those who want you to think they are the bomb. Follow Simon? Might as well ask if you'd follow David Koresh. Water is patient, it will take millions of years to carve out a valley, it will take its time to follow the winding streams back to the ocean. Water revives and preserves life. All of the organized religion stuff about who is in charge, who is respected, who is the leader, is something to run away from. Have as your Master the **Dharma**, humble, useful, kind, amplifying goodness and truth and peace and order, looking out what is best for all, and willing to evolve as needed.*

Kosalasamyutta 15 - - - - - - - - *A killer's child becomes a killer. A conqueror's child becomes a conqueror. An abuser's child becomes an abuser. A reviler's child becomes a reviler. The way that karma unfolds, the plunderer will eventually be plundered.*

John 8:38 I speak that which I have seen with [my] Father: and ye do that which ye have seen with your father.

Follow violent religious leaders and become violent fanatics. You don't have to become a child of that anymore. You are born again. You have a different Father now. Don't follow leaders if you don't wish to become like them.

Tao Te Ching 24 - - - - - - - - *You who **praise yourself** will not be respected by others. You who have discovered The Way will project no ego.*

Matthew 23:11-12 But he that is greatest among you shall be your servant. And whosoever shall exalt himself shall be abased; and he that shall humble himself shall be exalted.

It is a topsy-turvy world when it comes to spiritual advancement. Those who play the game of politics and insist on getting their way, who think God is on their side, who burn out like a flame and are forgotten, Simon and his Chosen People, will fade into footnotes of history books and archeological excavations. The anti-war weirdos who were just trying to escape the chaos of it all were to become the parents of one of the greatest religions of humanity, that of Christianity. Those who wished to fight Rome ended up crushed by Rome. Those who avoided the fight with Rome ended up defining the Roman Catholic Church, the Holy Roman Empire. The first became last while the last became first. There is no praise at the time for backing out of a holy war, it is unpatriotic, it is a lack of faith, it is a disgrace to the family, but these were the survivors.

Did I mention about half a million Jews died in the Third Jewish Roman War. That was a lot.

Those who think they should listen to the Brahmins

Culagopalaka Sutta 3 - - - - - - - - Unskilled in this world and in the other world, unskilled in Mara's (devil's) realm and what is beyond Mara's realm, unskilled in Death's realm and what is beyond Death's realm, it can only lead to the harm and suffering for a long time for those who think they should listen to the Brahmins (Hindu holy teachers) and place faith in them.

Lotus Sutra 02 - - - - - - - - - They are profound in that **commitment to wrong and useless doctrines**. *Clinging tightly to them, they cannot let them go.*

Matthew 23:13 But woe to you, scribes and Pharisees, hypocrites! Because you shut the kingdom of heaven against men; for you neither enter yourselves, nor allow those who would enter to go in.

Luke 11:52 Woe to you lawyers! For you have taken away the key of knowledge; you did not enter yourselves, and you hindered those who were entering."

Pharisees are a 2nd Century forward Jewish sect. There is no evidence of Pharisees dating back to the 1st Century. Every so often groups arise into popularity that present themselves as the experts and proceed to promote and support the worst advice they could have gathered. So much suffering has taken place because of religious fanatics, fundamentalist to some black and white logical position. Start the next crusade, the next witch hunt for the Inquisition, the destruction of writings and relics of alternative thoughts. The Pharisees were actually the liberals of their day. The outsider non-Jewish writer used them as a foil for the role of the Brahmins in the Buddhist stories. The point is not the actual historical Pharisee party and what they were like. They stand as a chorus in the play, a group opposing the protagonist Jesus much like the religious leaders of Thebes opposed Dionysus.

It seems it doesn't matter where you live or what century you live in, you will find a group that is your Brahmins, your Pharisees, your local establishment of organized "religion for profit" experts that don't like you going against their values and expertise. You have *something different to say. They have wrapped up the very concept of "religion" into a neat bundle to fleece the flock with and they don't need you to be competition. They don't need you telling anyone that they don't know what they're talking about. They don't need you presenting the evidence that it has all been lies, blind faith in ancient silly superstitions. They define God and heaven and how you can spiritually connect. They tell you that you are doomed for hell and then tell you they have the sacraments that will save you. The last thing that they want you to understand is that you have this **Gnosis**, this key of knowledge, that can propel you far beyond them.*

Dead body inside

Anangana Sutta 29 - - - - - - - - *Like a beautiful bronze dish, new from the shop, clean and bright, with a dead body inside, loathing, repugnant, disgusting.*

Matthew 23:25-26 Woe unto you, scribes and Pharisees, hypocrites! For ye make clean the outside of the cup and of the platter, but within they are full of extortion and excess. Thou blind Pharisee, cleanse first that which is within the cup and platter, that the outside of them may be clean also.

Various variations exist for the compromise "excess" used in the KJV: intemperance, unclean, covetousness, iniquity, unjust, wickedness. Organized religion, with its shiny stained glass windows and pretty ritual cups and plates, has been the heart of so many violent attacks on those considered and labeled as "evil" in its view. Inquisition, crusade, witch hunt.

The Catholic creation of the New Testament begins with the Jesus of Matthew, of peace and love, but it ends with Revelation and a Jesus of vengeance and the annihilation of the Romans. It has made for a schizophrenic religion that embraces both charity and crusades. Jesus loves you and onward Christian soldiers when the saints go marching in. That wasn't the original plan. That wasn't how the Gnostic version of Christianity was developing before it was snuffed out for being dangerous heresy.

Outwardly they are beautiful

Kosalasamyutta 11 - - - - - - - - *A person is not easily known by external appearance. A first impression should not be trusted. Some move about in disguise. Inwardly they are impure. Outwardly they are beautiful.*

Matthew 23:27-28 Woe unto you, scribes and Pharisees, hypocrites! For ye are like unto whited sepulchres, which indeed appear beautiful outward, but are within full of dead men's bones, and of all uncleanness. Even so ye also outwardly appear righteous unto men, but within ye are full of hypocrisy and iniquity.

It is unfortunately timeless and transcends cultures, people are not to be trusted, not what they appear. It is especially the "goody goody" people that you have to watch out for the most. It is the "extra nice" people that you will find have twisted your words against you and are your biggest problem even though they smile as they pass. It is the most faithful that start the holy wars.

False teachers who teach under the pretense of having authority

*Surangama Sutra - - - - - - - - In the End Times there will be false teachers who teach under the pretense of having authority, asserting that they have received their **Dharma** from a respected master, **deceiving ignorant people**.*

Matthew 24:23-25 Then if any man shall say unto you, Lo, here is Christ, or there; believe it not. For there shall arise false Christs, and false prophets, and shall shew great signs and wonders; insomuch that, if it were possible, they shall deceive the very elect. Behold, I have told you before.

Simon. Here is Messiah. Believe in him. Believe in the war effort surrounding him. Like a modern leader of a radical Islamic sect being surrounded by a network of terrorists, in jihad mode, Simon was much the same. The problem with someone being "Christ", being "Messiah", is that it comes with an obligation and expectation that there is a holy war to be fought and have faith in and sacrifice for and be willing to kill and die for, because God is obviously on their side.

The vast world will burn up

Anguttara Nikaya 7:62 - - - - - - - - The vast world will burn up, being completely destroyed and ceasing to exist.

Matthew 24:35 Heaven and earth shall pass away, but my words shall not pass away.

They want to conquer the world that won't last, while they miss out on the world that can never die.

How much do you get? How much can you pile up? Nothing will be forever. There is no promised land that will not one day be lost again to another invading people whose god has told them that it is now their promised land. There is no grand temple with golden treasures that will not one day be plundered, destroyed, and forgotten. In a hundred years, a thousand years, two thousand years, only the words remain, the ideas, the hopes and dreams and concepts to inspire and motivate people across the span of many cultures and languages and ages. Nothing else lasts. It all becomes at best monumental ruins for tourists or dig sites for archeologists. It is ideas that survive, scientific discoveries, music, collections of ideas, story characters and events that inspire across cultures and ages. In the beginning was the Word and the Word will outlive it all.

Stand by those who are the most in need

Mahavagga 8:26:3 - - - - - - - - Those who want to stand by me should stand by those who are the most in need.

Matthew 25:40   And the King shall answer and say unto them, Verily I say unto you, Inasmuch as ye have done it unto one of the least of these my brethren, ye have done it unto me.

Standing by the Messiah meant joining in with the holy war of the moment.   Standing by the Buddha means activating compassion for wherever it is needed.   The two ancient concepts are mutually exclusive.   You either have come to conquer and establish a kingdom of holy people, or you have come to invite everyone to participate in a kingdom not of this world.

The path of physical violence

Mahadukkhakkhakklandha Sutta 12 - - - - - - - - **Those who take swords** *and shields and buckle on bows and quivers, charging into battle with arrows and spears flying and swords flashing—they will be found run through with arrows and spears,* **their heads cut off by swords***.*

Kakacupama Sutta 20 - - - - - - - - *Even if bandits cut you limb from limb with a saw, the arising in the mind of hatred towards them would not be doing as I have taught you.*

Matthew 26:52 *Then said Jesus unto him, Put up again thy sword into his place: for all they that take the sword shall perish with the sword.*

In the story it was "Simon" who had taken up a sword to defend the concept of Messiah. Hatred and violence and xenophobia is not the way to change the world for the better.

Not of this world

Sela Sutta 16-17 - - - - - - - - *Buddha—**I am already a king**, Sela. I am supreme king of the **Dharma**. I rotate the **Dharma** wheel and no one can stop it from turning.*

Matthew 27:11   And Jesus stood before the governor: and the governor asked him, saying, Art thou the King of the Jews?   And Jesus said unto him, Thou sayest.

John 18:33-37   Then Pilate entered into the judgment hall again, and called Jesus, and said unto him, Art thou the King of the Jews? Jesus answered him, Sayest thou this thing of thyself, or did others tell it thee of me?   Pilate answered, Am I a Jew?   Thine own nation and the chief priests have delivered thee unto me: what hast thou done? Jesus answered, My kingdom is not of this world: if my kingdom were of this world, then would my servants fight, that I should not be delivered to the Jews: but now is my kingdom not from hence.   Pilate therefore said unto him, Art thou a king then?   Jesus answered, Thou sayest that I am a king.   To this end was I born, and for this cause came I into the world, that I should bear witness unto the truth.   Every one that is of the truth heareth my voice.

*A violent revolutionary leader becomes king if victorious.   It is conditional on winning the war.   A **Dharma** King is already a victor, already enthroned, ruling a kingdom not of this world.   The first to wear the title "Messiah" or "Christ" was King Saul, the first king of ancient Israel, the first king of the Jews.   Jesus is contrasted with that concept, not an earthly king, not a victorious Messiah come to conquer all of the enemies of the people.*

John alone preserves the response of Jesus.   In John it seems that Jesus denies being King of the Jews, denies being Christ of the Jews. His allegiance is of a kingdom beyond Judaea, beyond Judaism, even beyond any concept of God in this world.   His Father was the God above all the concepts of "God", the God beyond the cosmos, if we are to read the Gospel of John as the Marcionites would have.   He didn't want to be delivered to the Jews.   Not only not the Jewish Messiah, but not in any regards comrades with the Jews revolting against Rome.

A great earthquake occurred

Iddhipadasamyutta 10; Mahaparinibbana Sutta 6:10 - - - - - - - -
When the Blessed One had relinquished his vital formation, a **great**
earthquake occurred, *frightening and terrifying, and peals of thunder*
shook the sky.

Matthew 27:51   And, behold, the veil of the temple was rent in
twain from the top to the bottom; and the earth did quake, and the
rocks rent;

Earthquake denotes the death of the Buddha.   This links the Jesus
story back to the Buddhist traditions.

Bodies were glowing like the sun

Lotus Sutra 15 - - - - - - - - The ground of the billion lands of the enduring earth trembled and split open. **Out of it instantly emerged countless millions** *of bodhisattvas (saints) and mahasattvas (prophets). Their bodies were glowing like the sun.*

Matthew 27:52 And the graves were opened; and many bodies of the saints which slept arose,

The multitude of glowing zombies links the Jesus story to the Buddhist tradition. It symbolizes the unification of a tradition that goes back in time to the predecessors in the same spiritual movement. It makes for a good story telling visualization, but if historical there would have been more documented reports of such an amazing event.

The help of clear water

Vatthupama Sutta 12 - - - - - - - - *A cloth that is defiled and stained becomes pure and bright with the help of clear water.*

Matthew 28:19 Go ye therefore, and teach all nations, baptizing them in the name of the Father, and of the Son, and of the Holy Ghost:

Teach and immerse, spread the message to the world, Father Buddha has a Son, born of the Holy Spirit of the **Dharma***, bringing cleansing purity and renewed hope, returned peace and compassion and joy. Instead of a call to arms, a call to join the Messiah in revolution, this call is for a different kind of unification.*

I never become extinguished

*Lotus Sutra 16 - - - - - - - - At that time tell the sentient beings that I am here forever. I never become extinguished. Because of the necessity of an expedient means, at times I appear to be extinct, and at other times not. Know that as long as there are sentient beings in the many lands who are reverent and sincere in their desire to know, that I will be among them preaching the ultimate **Dharma**.*

Matthew 28:20 Teaching them to observe all things whatsoever I have commanded you: and, lo, I am with you I, even unto the end of the world.

*The ever-present Father figure. Jesus has this quality of **Gnosis** that embeds in the heart that is stronger than faith. For those who have this **Jesus Gnosis**, there is no taking it away. It could be proven that none of it was historically real, none of it actually happened, and Jesus never existed in the way that Sunday School explained the stories, but such proven would not take the **Gnosis** of Jesus out of the hearts of those who have made the link. The world will end, with all its politics and money and religion and logic. It will end many times over. There are a few ideas that transcend, that are as valid today as in a thousand years and as valid here is a thousand miles away. These ideas are alive and will reappear even if all the words are lost. Ideas like compassion and acceptance and peace and serenity and forgiveness and humility form a living **Dharma** that transcends planets and species and universes and time.*

Mansions beyond

Maratajjaniya Sutta 25 - - - - - - - - *In the heart of the sea there are mansions that last for aeons—sapphires shining with a fiery gleaming clear translucent luster where iridescent sea nymphs dance in beautiful intricate patterns.*

Lotus Sutra 14 - - - - - - - - *When I have attained supreme perfect awakening, in the place where I will be, I will engage the powers of* **transcending wisdom to draw you to myself** *and cause you to remain within my* **Dharma**.

Mahasihanada Sutta 41 - - - - - - - - *On the dissolution of the body, the holy person will reappear in a* **happy destination**, *in the heavenly world, experiencing extremely pleasant feelings, as a man on a path directed to a mansion with lofty finished rooms and comfortable furnishings.*

John 14:2-4 In my Father's house are many mansions: if it were not so, I would have told you. I go to prepare a place for you. And if I go and prepare a place for you, I will come again, and receive you unto myself; that where I am, there ye may be also. And whither I go ye know, and the way ye know.

In a lot of spiritual traditions there is the idea of an ultimate destination that will welcome home those who have found the way to get there. Paradise, heaven, the Gnostic concept of completion (Pleroma), the Buddhist concept of emptiness (Nirvana), all offer a light at the end of the tunnel, a happy destination.

Culasaccaka Sutta 26 - - - - - - - - **The Blessed One has attained Nirvana** *and he teaches the* **Dharma** *for attaining Nirvana.*

John 14:6 Jesus saith unto him, I am the way, the truth, and the life: no man cometh unto the Father, but by me.

Khandhasamyutta 87 - - - - - - - - *Why do you want to see my foul body? You who see the* **Dharma** *see me. You who see me see the* **Dharma**.

John 14:9 Jesus saith unto him, Have I been so long time with you, and yet hast thou not known me, Philip? he that hath seen me hath seen the Father; and how sayest thou then, Shew us the Father?

The exit door

Khandhasamyutta 94 - - - - - - - - *As a lotus flower is born in the water and grows up in the water, but having risen up above the water, it stands without a spot of the water, you are born in the world, grew up in the world, but having overcome the world, **stand without a spot of the world**.*

Anenjasappaya Sutta 03 - - - - - - - - *Live with an abundant and exalted state of mind, **transcending the world in your firm determination**. Doing so, there are no more evil unwholesome mental states. No greed. No ill will. No presumption. Abandoning these states achieve a state of mind that is unlimited, immeasurable, and well developed.*

Lankavatara 11 - - - - - - - - *The resurrection from mortal body to transcendental body does not involve mortal death. The old body continues to live and the old mind serves its needs, but it is now freed from mortal thinking. There has occurred **an inconceivable transforming death**.*

John 17:14-17 I have given them thy word; and the world hath hated them, because they are not of the world, even as I am not of the world. I pray not that thou shouldest take them out of the world, but that thou shouldest keep them from the evil. They are not of the world, even as I am not of the world. Sanctify them through thy truth: thy word is truth.

You come to a point where you can no longer play their game anymore. Their whole circus is meaningless to you. You are dead to them. You are not pulled along with greed for what they want you to want. You are not convinced to fear and hate those they want you to be against. You no longer accept their lies and manipulations as accurate histories and disclosed honesty. The "world" out there is made up of mental constructs of people and institutions that want to check and control your views, your reactions, your words, your actions, your contracts, your religion, your collection of wise conclusions, and your very self-identity. Once you snap out of that matrix, you can never fit yourself back in.

The word discovered is not of this world, not of the human cultural religious traditional system in play. The word resonates in the mind isolated from the herd, left alone on a vision quest, at the *inner sanctuary where we all become true to ourselves and ask ourselves the important questions. This **Dharma**, this **Gnosis**, this Holy Spirit found, becomes the inner light, the inner spring, the inner voice, that is stronger than any influence of any person or institution out there. It makes you into a monk who can stroll through town but can never be a normal citizen there ever again.*

Defend yourself from participating in the war. Defend yourself from participating in their divisions, their fears and hates, their greed and thirst for conquest, their violence and destruction, their imaginary lines drawn, their imaginary goals sought, their imaginary unstoppable hero Messiah, their chosen people xenophobia exclusiveness, and their limited concept of God.

*Lotus Sutra 02 - - - - - - - - I took my vow of hope **to make all persons like me**, without any distinctions to be made between us.*

John 17:22-23 And the glory which thou gavest me I have given them; that they may be one, even as we are one: I in them, and thou in me, that they may be made perfect in one; and that the world may know that thou hast sent me, and hast loved them, as thou hast loved me.

For the disciple to be like Buddha, like Jesus, one with his oneness, complete with his completion, perfect with his perfection, integrated into the sameness, is a mystical concept not at home in Western thinking. There is this division between God and humanity, immortal and dying, divine and mundane, and the "Jesus" of Christianity is cast into this "God beyond us" category and we are but the lowly disciples. There is a thought in Gnostic circles that Jesus pointed out the way and the Christians stopped to worship his pointing finger instead of following the instructions. Awakened wants all to be awakened. Enlightened wants all to be enlightened. Experienced wants all to be experienced. Once you see the exit door to the burning building, you want everyone to know about it.

*Lotus Sutra 08 - - - - - - - - Preaching the Law (**Dharma**) in a way that makes it clear and pure, there will remain no doubts and no confusions [...] Of the Buddha's limitless treasure, we have collected only a fraction of Nirvana, having deluded ourselves into thinking it to be enough.*

John 21:25 And there are also many other things which Jesus did, the which, if they should be written every one, I suppose that even

*the world itself could not contain the books that should be written.
Amen.*

Hope

Bhaddali Sutta 30 - - - - - - - - *Those who have become are fading away and the true* **Dharma** *is vanishing.*

Lotus Sutra 14 - - - - - - - - *And afterward he will enter Nirvana, like the ending of the smoke after a lamp has been extinguished. In that evil age to follow, one who preaches this ultimate* **Dharma** *will be truly blessed.*

John 12:35-36   Then Jesus said unto them, Yet a little while is the light with you. Walk while ye have the light, lest darkness come upon you: for he that walketh in darkness knoweth not whither he goeth. While ye have light, believe in the light, that ye may be the children of light. These things spake Jesus, and departed, and did hide himself from them.

The hiding away of Jesus is symbolic, as is the extinguishing of the light, the lost and confused world stumbling in the dark, not knowing which direction to go. It is the way of spirituality for the few to glimpse into the Answer while the many are lost in their own mind games. That leaves it up to those who have kindled the light within to shine it as we can and do the best we can. A legion of soldiers is not going to halt for one child holding up a flower. But perhaps a time of peace will one day appear in which these words will be appreciated and enlighten future generations.

Appendix 1: The Original Jesus Christ

Jesus

Joshua 1:14 Your wives, your little ones, and your cattle, shall remain in the land which Moses gave you on this side Jordan; but ye shall pass before your brethren armed, all the mighty men of valour, and help them;

Joshua 3:1 And Joshua rose early in the morning; and they removed from Shittim, and came to Jordan, he and all the children of Israel, and lodged there before they passed over.

Joshua in Hebrew (Yehoshuwa), Jesus in Greek (Iesous), was the name of the fabled ancient Jewish hero that led the Chosen People across the Jordan River into their Promised Land. The name became symbolic for the hope of a leader who could make Israel great again. The name means salvation, so everywhere in the Jewish scriptures that the concept of salvation was presented could be interpreted as a prophecy about this coming savior, leader, deliverer. Thus "Jesus" can be a title, a label, more so than just a proper name.

Christ

1 Samuel 2:10 The adversaries of the LORD shall be broken to pieces; out of heaven shall he thunder upon them: the LORD shall judge the ends of the earth; and he shall give strength unto his king, and exalt the horn of his anointed.

*1 Samuel 15:17-18 And Samuel said, When thou wast little in thine own sight, wast thou not made the head of the tribes of Israel, and the LORD **anointed** thee king over Israel? And the LORD sent thee on a journey, and said, Go and utterly destroy the sinners the Amalekites, and fight against them until they be consumed.*

Messiah in Hebrew (Mashiyach), Christ in Greek (Christos), was the title of the ruling king, meaning anointed one, first applied to king Saul. The same word is sometimes left as Messiah or changed to Anointed. The original Hebrew does not have this English blurring. After the fall of Jerusalem in 135, the Rabbinical form of Judaism began speaking about the Messiah in spiritual terms, of a Messianic age to come. After the rise of Roman Catholic Christianity, Christ was seen as the Son of God who had ascended into heaven and will one day come back again. Up through the defeat of Simon bar Kokhba, the concept of Christ, of Messiah, was that of a victorious warrior king, a very real and human hero backed by God. It is this hero warrior that was meant whenever anyone was referred to as Christian at this time, whenever the label of Christ was applied to anyone. There was no being "Christ" without having a plan to defeat the occupation of the Romans and the corruption of Hellenism and other foreign forms of philosophy and religion. The image of the Jesus of Matthew standing on a mountain top preaching about peace and forgiveness and tolerance and compassion would have been seen at the time as having absolutely nothing to do with representing "Jesus" or representing "Christ", nothing to do with representing "Joshua" or representing "Messiah".

Jesus Christ 1.0

The combination "Jesus Christ" or "Joshua Messiah" was code for the Chosen People will regain the Promised Land and destroy the Romans who want to stand in their way. This was changed with the way Christianity turned out, but there are still echoes of the original meaning. The final text in the New Testament of the Catholic Bible is Revelation, which predates the Gospel when looking at all of this through my lens of focus. This was a pre-135 Jesus Christ, full of piss and vinegar and lots of visions of bloodshed and world domination.

Revelation 1:1 The Revelation of Jesus Christ, which God gave unto him, to shew unto his servants things which must shortly come to pass; and he sent and signified it by his angel unto his servant John:

This was designed to be propaganda support for joining a cosmic battle brought to life, the Armageddon apocalypse of destruction of the Beast of the world and the coming new age for the faithful servants.

Revelation 11:15 And the seventh angel sounded; and there were great voices in heaven, saying, The kingdoms of this world are become the kingdoms of our Lord, and of his Christ; and he shall reign for ever and ever.

The revolution to take place was from "this world" having taken over, the Roman Empire and the Hellenism philosophies, to a new era in which the Christ rules as king.

Revelation 12:17 And the dragon was wroth with the woman, and went to make war with the remnant of her seed, which keep the commandments of God, and have the testimony of Jesus Christ.

Jesus Christ is a symbol of faith and hope for the Chosen People with the only true religion of the only true god, and anything that opposes this is demonized and labeled as sinners to be destroyed.

Revelation 20:4 And I saw thrones, and they sat upon them, and judgment was given unto them: and I saw the souls of them that were beheaded for the witness of Jesus, and for the word of God, and which had not worshipped the beast, neither his image, neither had received his mark upon their foreheads, or in their hands; and they lived and reigned with Christ a thousand years.

Those who fight with the Christ, the Messiah, will reign with him once the foreign "beast" is defeated. The "beast" that wanted to be worshipped was one of the Caesars who customarily had a statue erected and were promoted to the status of being a demigod. The forehead marks probably indicated Jews who fought for the Romans instead of for the Christ factions. In both the wars in 66 and 132, Roman records show Jewish names in the lists of soldiers who worked in the Legions.

Revelation 20:6 Blessed and holy is he that hath part in the first resurrection: on such the second death hath no power, but they shall be priests of God and of Christ, and shall reign with him a thousand years.

The idea that being a martyr brought with it reward inspires suicide bombers to this day. This idea of a Jesus Christ supporting violence against the Devil's World has caused so much suffering and destruction and injustice and fear throughout centuries of time. Crusades and inquisitions and witch hunts echo from the Dark Ages through the Enlightenment. Ending the Bible on such a message is at least in part at fault. I think "the Sermon on the Mount Jesus Christ" was the antidote, the correction, the **Jesus 2.0** *that everyone should have upgraded to but didn't.*

Kokhba

Numbers 24:17 I shall see him, but not now: I shall behold him, but not nigh: there shall come a Star out of Jacob, and a Sceptre shall *rise out of Israel, and shall **smite** the corners of Moab, and **destroy** all the children of Sheth.*

Kowkab in Hebrew is star, another code word for the coming Messiah.

Matthew 2:2 Saying, Where is he that is born King of the Jews? for we have seen his star in the east, and are come to worship him.

Where is the Star Child who will grow up to bring about a new kingdom for Jews? He has already been born. It is only a matter of time now.

*Revelation 2:26-28 And he that overcometh, and keepeth my works unto the end, to him will I give **power over the nations**: And he shall rule them with a rod of iron; as the vessels of a potter shall they be broken to shivers: even as I received of my Father. And I will give him the morning star.*

Keep the faith, fight the fight, and the star will appear, the Messiah you hope for.

Revelation 8:10-11 And the third angel sounded, and there fell a great star from heaven, burning as it were a lamp, and it fell upon the third part of the rivers, and upon the fountains of waters; And the name of the star is called Wormwood: and the third part of the waters became wormwood; and many men died of the waters, because they were made bitter.

The Romans built aqueducts and baths. For the star to pollute the water is symbolic of being defiant to Roman initiated changes.

Revelation 9:1-4 And the fifth angel sounded, and I saw a star fall from heaven unto the earth: and to him was given the key of the bottomless pit. And he opened the bottomless pit; and there arose a smoke out of the pit, as the smoke of a great furnace; and the sun and the air were darkened by reason of the smoke of the pit. And there came out of the smoke locusts upon the earth: and unto them was given power, as the scorpions of the earth have power. And it was commanded them that they should not hurt the grass of the earth, neither any green thing, neither any tree; but only those men which have not the seal of God in their foreheads.

The Christ people, the Messianic revolutionaries backing Simon the Star, hid in underground caves, came out using guerilla warfare tactics against the Romans and against any Jew who did not support the revolution.

Revelation 22:16 I Jesus have sent mine angel to testify unto you these things in the churches. I am the root and the offspring of David, and the bright and morning star.

Churches is Ecclesia in Greek, a gathering assembly of people, an appropriate name for places where volunteers would join the resistance movement. To bringing back the greatness of David's Israel in joining with the Star.

Violence

Matthew 10:34-40 Think not that I am come to send peace on earth: I came not to send peace, but a sword. For I am come to set a man at variance against his father, and the daughter against her mother, and the daughter in law against her mother in law. And a man's foes shall be they of his own household. He that loveth father or mother more than me is not worthy of me: and he that loveth son or daughter more than me is not worthy of me. And he that taketh not his cross, and followeth after me, is not worthy of me. He that findeth his life shall lose it: and he that loseth his life for my sake shall find it. He that receiveth you receiveth me, and he that receiveth me receiveth him that sent me.

Ezekiel 18:19-21 Yet say ye, Why? doth not the son bear the iniquity of the father? When the son hath done that which is lawful and right, and hath kept all my statutes, and hath done them, he shall surely live. The soul that sinneth, it shall die. The son shall not bear the iniquity of the father, neither shall the father bear the iniquity of the son: the righteousness of the righteous shall be upon him, and the wickedness of the wicked shall be upon him. But if the wicked will turn from all his sins that he hath committed, and keep all my statutes, and do that which is lawful and right, he shall surely live, he shall not die.

Return and Revival of Promised Land

Unity through submission, through repentance of everything that makes you different, through blind faith agreement to believe and think and react and speak and live and identify with and support the one true way of thinking. Or die. Purified unity. The Messiah is to serve and protect the Purified unity of the Chosen People in the Promised Land against all outside demonic forces (foreign governments and philosophies). Messiah's role is to restore political sovereignty for Israel.

Hosea 3:4-5 For the children of Israel shall abide many days without a king, and without a prince, and without a sacrifice, and without an image, and without an ephod, and without teraphim: Afterward shall the children of Israel return, and seek the LORD their God, and David their king; and shall fear the LORD and his goodness in the latter days.

The servitude status of Israel to foreign kingdoms is the reason the Messiah comes. Jerusalem having Romans living there as rulers over the suppressed and occupied Jewish people, with its foreign gods, foreign customs, and disrespect for the sacred uniqueness of the god of Israel, was a rally cry for looking for the prophesized Messiah to come.

*Amos 9:8-15 Behold, the eyes of the Lord GOD are upon the sinful kingdom, and I will destroy it from off the face of the earth; saving that I will not utterly destroy the house of Jacob, saith the LORD. For, lo, I will command, and I will sift the house of Israel among all nations, like as corn is sifted in a sieve, yet shall not the least grain fall upon the earth. All the sinners of my people shall die by the sword, which say, The evil shall not overtake nor prevent us. In that day will I raise up the tabernacle of David that is fallen, and close up the breaches thereof; and I will raise up his ruins, and I will build it as in the days of old: That they may possess the remnant of Edom, and of all the heathen, which are called by my name, saith the LORD that doeth this. Behold, the days come, saith the LORD, that the plowman shall overtake the reaper, and the treader of grapes him that soweth seed; and the mountains shall drop sweet wine, and all the hills shall melt. And I will bring again the captivity of my people of Israel, and **they shall build the waste cities, and inhabit them**; and they shall plant vineyards, and drink the wine thereof; they shall also make gardens, and eat the fruit of them. And I will plant them upon their land, and they shall no more be pulled up out of their land which I have given them, saith the LORD thy God.*

Jeremiah 23:3-5 And I will gather the remnant of my flock out of all countries whither I have driven them, and will bring them again to their folds; and they shall be fruitful and increase. And I will set up shepherds over them which shall feed them: and they shall fear no more, nor be dismayed, neither shall they be lacking, saith the LORD.

Behold, the days come, saith the LORD, that I will raise unto David a righteous Branch, and a King shall reign and prosper, and shall execute judgment and justice in the earth.

Jeremiah 30:3   For, lo, the days come, saith the LORD, that I will bring again the captivity of my people Israel and Judah, saith the LORD: and I will cause them to return to the land that I gave to their fathers, and they shall possess it.

Jeremiah 30:8-10   For it shall come to pass in that day, saith the LORD of hosts, that I will break his yoke from off thy neck, and will burst thy bonds, and strangers shall no more serve themselves of him: But they shall serve the LORD their God, and David their king, whom I will raise up unto them.   Therefore fear thou not, O my servant Jacob, saith the LORD; neither be dismayed, O Israel: for, lo, I will save thee from afar, and thy seed from the land of their captivity; and Jacob shall return, and shall be in rest, and be quiet, and none shall make him afraid.

Isaiah 11:1-4   And there shall come forth a rod out of the stem of Jesse, and a Branch shall grow out of his roots: And the spirit of the LORD shall rest upon him, the spirit of wisdom and understanding, the spirit of counsel and might, the spirit of knowledge and of the fear of the LORD; And shall make him of quick understanding in the fear of the LORD: and he shall not judge after the sight of his eyes, neither reprove after the hearing of his ears: But with righteousness shall he judge the poor, and reprove with equity for the meek of the earth: and he shall smite the earth with the rod of his mouth, and with the breath of his lips shall he slay the wicked.

These "prophecies" apply to someone like Simon bar Kokhba, not to the peace and love Jesus preaching his Sermon on the Mount. Smiting and slaying are not properties of the Dharma.

Appendix 2: Dio's Account

Cassius Dio Cocceianus recorded in the year 222 in his Roman History, book 69, 12-14:

At Jerusalem he founded a city in place of the one which had been razed to the ground, naming it Aelia Capitolina, and on the site of the temple of the god he raised a new temple to Jupiter. This brought on a war of no slight importance nor of brief duration, for the Jews deemed it intolerable that foreign races should be settled in their city and foreign religious rites planted there. So long, indeed, as Hadrian was close by in Egypt and again in Syria, they remained quiet, save in so far as they purposely made of poor quality such weapons as they were called upon to furnish, in order that the Romans might reject them and they themselves might thus have the use of them; but when he went farther away, they openly revolted. To be sure, they did not dare try conclusions with the Romans in the open field, but they occupied the advantageous positions in the country and strengthened them with mines and walls, in order that they might have places of refuge whenever they should be hard pressed, and might meet together unobserved underground; and they pierced these subterranean passages from above at intervals to let in air and light.

At first the Romans took no account of them. Soon, however, all Judaea had been stirred up, and the Jews everywhere were showing signs of disturbance, were gathering together, and giving evidence of great hostility to the Romans, partly by secret and partly by overt acts; many outside nations, too, were joining them through eagerness for gain, and the whole earth, one might almost say, was being stirred up over the matter. Then, indeed, Hadrian sent against them his best generals. First of these was Julius Severus, who was dispatched from Britain, where he was governor, against the Jews. Severus did not venture to attack his opponents in the open at any one point, in view of their numbers and their desperation, but by intercepting small groups, thanks to the number of his soldiers and his under-officers, and by depriving them of food and shutting them up, he was able, rather slowly, to be sure, but with comparatively little danger, to crush, exhaust and exterminate them. Very few of them in fact survived.

Fifty of their most important outposts and nine hundred and eighty-five of their most famous villages were razed to the ground. Five hundred and eighty thousand men were slain in the various raids and battles, and the number of those that perished by famine, disease and fire was past finding out. Thus nearly the whole of Judaea was made desolate, a result of which the people had had forewarning before the war. For the tomb of Solomon, which the Jews regard as an object of veneration, fell to pieces of itself and collapsed, and many wolves and hyenas rushed howling into their cities. Many Romans, moreover, perished in this war. Therefore, Hadrian in writing to the senate did not employ the opening phrase commonly affected by the emperors, "If you and our children are in health, it is well; I and the legions are in health."

Appendix 3: Gnostic Texts

Barabbas

Matthew 27:16-17 And they had then a notable prisoner, called [Jesus] Barabbas. Therefore when they were gathered together, Pilate said unto them, Whom will ye that I release unto you? Barabbas, or Jesus which is called Christ?

Bar-abbas means son of the father.

The name "Jesus" was removed and today there are only 6 Greek, 1 Armenian, and 2 Syrian versions that preserve "Jesus" in this verse. Now why was the distinction and choice given here between killing or freeing "Jesus, Son of the Father" and "Jesus, Christ of the Jews"? Could the "Christ of the Jews" be a reference to one or all of the Messianic pretenders like Simon bar Kokhba? Which Messianic tradition do you people want? Was he the authentic heir to the tradition of xenophobia and terrorist style revolutionary movements? Or was he the "Son of the Father" teacher of pacifist openness to interracial harmony and a spiritual mindset that can transcend Judaism? There is something confusing going on in the very question. Is the question who should come in between the Jews and the Romans? They chose Jesus Christ (Simon bar Kokhba) to take the path of violence straight to his certain death at the hands of the Romans. They let disappear into the night Jesus Barabbas, the voice of reason and compromise, of wisdom and peace.

Matthew 27:24-25 When Pilate saw that he could prevail nothing, but that rather a tumult was made, he took water, and washed his hands before the multitude, saying, I am innocent of the blood of this just person: see ye to it. Then answered all the people, and said, His blood be on us, and on our children.

If the rest of Hadrian's career as Emperor of Rome is any indication, he would have preferred to have ended the conflict with the Jews, negotiated peace, stopped the bloodshed and death, helped them rebuild. It was the Jews who insisted that the Roman Legions kill "Jesus Christ 1.0", kill Simon bar Kokhba, the self-proclaimed king of the Jews, the one chosen to confront them.

*Mark 15:21-23 And they compel one **Simon a Cyrenian**, who passed by, coming out of the country, the father of Alexander and*

*Rufus, **to bear his cross**. And they bring him unto the place Golgotha, which is, being interpreted, The place of a skull. And they gave him to drink wine mingled with myrrh: but he received it not.*

*Mark 15:25 And it was the third hour, and **they crucified him**.*

Simon (Simon bar Kokhba) a Cyrenian (Cyrene was one of the main sites of the Jewish instigated violence in the Kitos War), was to bear the cross. He was offered wine (a peace treaty) but refused it. The third hour (three years into the war) Simon was killed. The year was 135.

Basilides explained that it was all an allegory, none of it literally happened, and that it was Simon who died on the cross while the real Jesus was sitting on the hill looking down and laughing.

Second Treatise of the Great Seth

Three Nag Hammadi preserved Gnostic texts are worth considering in the light of what we have been studying. The first quote is from a Sethian Gnostic text. Seth is the third son of humanity, the third child of Adam and Eve, from the ancient Jewish text typically known as Genesis. When the first two sons failed, one having died and the other having gone away in exile, the third son, Seth, carried on the fate of humanity. The Gnostic Jesus was identified with Seth.

*NHL VII 55:30 For my death, which they think happened, (happened) to them in their error and blindness, since **they nailed their man unto their death**. For their Ennoias did not see me, for they were deaf and blind. But in doing these things, they condemn themselves. Yes, they saw me; they punished me. It was another, their father, who drank the gall and the vinegar; it was not I. They struck me with the reed; it was another, **Simon, who bore the cross on his shoulder**. I was another upon Whom they placed the crown of thorns. But I was rejoicing in the height over all the wealth of the archons and the offspring of their error, of their empty glory. And **I was laughing at their ignorance**.*

NHL VII 64:18 For the Archon was a laughingstock because he said, "I am God, and there is none greater than I. I alone am the Father, the Lord, and there is no other beside me. I am a jealous God. And the senseless and blind ones are always senseless, always being slaves of law and earthly fear. And do not become female, lest you give birth to evil and (its) brothers: jealousy and division, anger and wrath, fear and a divided heart, and empty, non-existent desire. But I am an ineffable mystery to you.

*In Greek drama, an unexpected twist was often used, cases of mistaken identity, reversals, shifts of realization that the initial guess of the audience was wrong and that they had to see things in a different way to understand the plot. Notice it doesn't say they nailed their man unto his death. Their choice led to their own death, a death brought about by their being deaf and blind senseless slaves of an absurd ancient religion of rules and fear. Of all the gods in the Roman Empire, their god dares to wish to be the only one, the greatest one. He rallies his faithful like Mars, giving them the cross to bear of his jealously and vengeance on all who dare to question his supremacy. Don't be his female. Don't be his bitch, or you will give birth to jealousy, exclusiveness, "your ideas and only yours", division, judgement, anger, wrath, fear, the insane urge to lash out in violence, cold logic without compassion. Is this what you wish to give birth to, to present to the next generation? Or do you sit back and laugh at their ignorance and be comforted by the **Gnosis** that makes you not think like them?*

Thomas the Contender

*NHL II 143:8 Then the savior continued, saying, **"Woe to you, godless ones, who have no hope, who rely on things that will not happen**! Woe to you who hope in the flesh and in the prison that will perish! How long will you be oblivious? And how long will you suppose that the imperishables will perish too? Your hope is set upon the world, and your god is this life! You are corrupting your souls! **Woe to you within the fire that burns in you, for it is insatiable**! Woe to you because of the wheel that turns in your minds! Woe to you within the grip of the burning that is in you, for it will devour your flesh openly and rend your souls secretly, and prepare you for your companions! Woe to you, captives, for **you are bound in caverns**! You laugh! In mad laughter you rejoice! You neither realize your perdition, nor do you reflect on your circumstances, nor have you understood that you dwell in darkness and death! On the contrary, you are drunk with the fire and full of bitterness. Your mind is deranged on account of the burning that is in you, and sweet to you* *are the poison and the blows of your enemies! And the darkness rose for you like the light, for you surrendered your freedom for servitude! You darkened your hearts and surrendered your thoughts to folly, and you filled your thoughts with the smoke of the fire that is in you! And your light has hidden in the cloud of [...] and the garment that is put upon you, you [...]. And you were seized by the hope that does not exist. And whom is it you have believed? Do you not know that you all dwell among those who that [...] you as though you [...]. You baptized your souls in the water of darkness! You walked by your own whims!*

To me, this speaks of Simon's people hiding in underground tunnels and still having faith. They are so determined that they would prefer a life of being terrorists than to give up the burning quest for their Messianic dream. The Thomas the Contender text is about those who can see another way, a god above the god of jealous war, a clear air up above the smoke and dust. Those who have such **Gnosis** of such are not respected, not listened to, not esteemed teachers. Thomas asks the Savior how he can get the message across to them, when they only ridicule and have contempt and misunderstand. The quiet voices of the new Christianity had to wait until the old Christianity burned itself out. After Simon the Christ (Messiah) and the half million faithful lay dead in the midst of a thousand destroyed towns, then the alternative meek and mild Sermon on the Mount Christ 2.0 could have a chance to inspire new generations.

Apocalypse of Peter

*NHL VII 81:3   When he had said those things, I saw him seemingly being seized by them. And I said "What do I see, O Lord? That it is you yourself whom they take, and that you are grasping me? Or **who is this one, glad and laughing on the tree**? And is it another one whose feet and hands they are striking?" The Savior said to me, "He whom you saw on the tree, glad and laughing, this is **the living Jesus**. But this one into whose hands and feet they drive the nails is his fleshly part, which is the substitute being put to shame, the one who came into being in his likeness. But look at him and me." But I, when I had looked, said "Lord, no one is looking at you. Let us flee this place." But he said to me, "I have told you, 'Leave the blind alone!'. And you, see how they do not know what they are saying. For* *the son of their glory instead of my servant, they have put to shame." And I saw someone about to approach us resembling him, even him who was laughing on the tree. And he was <filled> with a Holy Spirit, and he is the Savior. And there was a great, ineffable light around them, and the multitude of ineffable and invisible angels blessing them. And when I looked at him, the one who gives praise was revealed. And he said to me, "Be strong, for you are the one to whom these mysteries have been given, to know them through revelation, that **he whom they crucified is the first-born, and the home of demons, and the stony vessel in which they dwell, of Elohim, of the cross, which is under the Law.** But he who stands near him is the living Savior, the first in him, whom they seized and released, who stands joyfully looking at those who did him violence, while they are divided among themselves.*

*The Passion story of the Gospel was originally presented as a Greek play, a commentary on the selection between the son of Jewish glory, Simon, and the Savior alternative wise spirit of radiant light. It was expected that Simon would blow his trumpet and angels would fly from the sky to assist him in his battles. It was the Savior that was seen to be surrounded by angelic beings. While the two options may look like twins, it is only because people are too blind to see the differences. At the start of the play, the twist was presented that the wrong man was executed, but by the end of the play the audience understands that his death was part of a greater plot to propel us into the understanding of the Mysteries of the Fullness (Pleroma) of **Gnosis**. The old religion had to die before there becomes room for the new religion to transform us.*

The play opened in Aelia Capitolina in the newly constructed theatre in the year 135. It received a standing ovation.

After Word

People are not shouting about peace so much if their world is peaceful. People are not shouting about compassion if their world is full of empathy. Peace and love become the mantras of war, for those who don't feel the patriotism, who don't have faith in the savior presented, who are sick and tired of the violence and destruction. There is no counter-culture without the status quo culture being broken, no antidote without a disease to cure, no solution without a problem to address. There is no awaiting dawn without it still being dark out. There is no calming of the storm without their having been a storm.

A peace and love Jesus on the mountain stands in stark contrast to the Messianic expectation of a hero to appear to defeat all of the foreign faces, to eliminate all of the signs of foreigners ever being present, to usher in a golden age of victory for the traditional values unique to the Chosen People in their Promised Land. Simon is underground hiding in silence and here we have Jesus on the mountain top in plain view shouting to the world. The son of man is in contrast to the Great Messiah, the son of God, the hero that everyone has blind faith in.

There stand three great forces at play: religion, politics, and the people. Their world is at war, conflict defined, sides chosen, faith put to the test. Religion is locked in place, determined. Politics is organized and ready for battles to begin. But who will the people back? Who will they select as their representative to face the Mighty Romans? Who is their David to challenge such a Goliath? Will they turn over their children to the war machine? Will they pledge their faith and patriotism? Will they follow the son of God into war? Who to abandon and who to send into the mission? Who to dismiss and who to condemn to the fate?

The most dangerous voice in the midst of war is the one shouting for peace. Who is this trouble maker, turning the tables, upsetting the machine, questioning the authority of the decisions and recommendations of the high priest and all of the wisest of spiritual teachers and leaders? What does this simple son of man have to contribute in teaching the world about peace and love? That we can cooperate and celebrate the differences? Satan has taken over his mind. Love our enemies? The sacred scriptures demand that we stand and fight. Shift our identity and thought into a cosmopolitan scope and leave xenophobia as a relic of a past age? Christ forbid! Send Simon to face the Romans head on. God will not forsake him.

Speculation is interesting. You can play "what if" games of ponderings. You can consider things that you can never prove, but at the same time they cannot be disproven. So little time, so much to unlearn. The "what if" of this round of key strokes called a book is ultimately about the possibility that the Gospel was created as a response to the defeat of Simon in 135, filling a void for those who had lost hopes in their Messianic dreams and needed a different kind of hero to admire and follow.

So here are the pieces to the puzzle. Hadrian in Alexandria discovering the **Dharma**. *Basic who and where and what. Basic creative ability and motive and influence. Cherish peace and he set out to actively end military conflicts. Cherish charity and he set out to help people across his Empire. Cherish Wisdom and he build libraries and temples to exercise the minds and spirits of people. Cherish* **Dharma** *and create Gospel? A way to negotiate peace, defuse the violent Christ concept and replace it with a Western Buddha, a Stoic teacher of Jews who could listen to reason. If Hadrian didn't sponsor the Gospel project, if he ever sat in his Alexandrian style garden in Rome in his solitary contemplative style and read the Sermon on the Mount, he would have appreciated the syncretic brilliance and cosmopolitan and timeless collection of truths that would long outlive the memory of anything he had accomplished in his days of being Caesar.*

Peace and love

Pax quies otium tranquillitas animi.

Amor caritas dilectio ardor complexus affectus eros venus gratia pietas.

www.ingramcontent.com/pod-product-compliance
Lightning Source LLC
Chambersburg PA
CBHW031200270326
41931CB00006B/345